Just for Kids

The New England Guide & Activity Book

by Ed and Roon Frost

illustrated by Carol Leach

For Young Travelers

Glove Compartment Books
P.O. Box 1602
Portsmouth, NH 03801

Ed Frost is a New Englander by birth and choice. He enjoys traveling with his family. Together with his wife, he has written two books for adults, COAST GUIDE and MOUNTAIN GUIDE, both published by Glove Compartment Books. The Frosts live in Eliot, ME with their son.

A freelance writer for fourteen years, Roon Frost has had a byline in a wide range of national and regional publications. In addition to travel writing, she coauthored THE LITTLE BOY BOOK, published by Ballantine and Clarkson N. Potter, Inc.

Artist Carol Leach, who lives in Kittery, ME, has her own line of greeting cards for kids and sew-your-own dolls. An elementary-school teacher for almost ten years, she has also illustrated books, consulted for a children's museum, and worked as a juvenile bookstore manager.

Cover design of Ms. Leach's pencil drawing is by Francesca Mastrangelo, who operates Angel Graphic Design Studio, Portsmouth, NH. Her work has appeared in numerous New England magazines, such as New Hampshire Profiles and Seacoast Life.

Educator and author Sheila Moore served as a consultant on this book. In addition, special thanks go to all the children and teachers who completed or reviewed different activities and stories.

Dawn Ronco, who runs Integrated Graphics in Lee, NH, is responsible for editing and lay-out of "Places to Go."

Typesetting provided by Portsmouth's Ligature Typography, quality advertising and book typographers.

FIRST EDITION

JUST FOR KIDS: THE NEW ENGLAND GUIDE AND ACTIVITY BOOK FOR YOUNG TRAVELERS. Copyright 1989 by Ed and Roon Frost. All rights reserved. Printed in the United States of America. No part of this book may be used or reproduce in any manner whatsoever without written permission except in the case of brief quotations embodied in critical articles or reviews. For information, address Glove Compartment Books, PO Box 1602, Portsmouth, NH 03801-1602.

ISBN 0-9618806-2-7

To order, contact:
    Independent Publishers Group
    814 North Franklin Street
    Chicago, IL 60610
    1-800/888-4741
Please include $2 for postage and handling.

Table of Contents

A Travel Guide that is "Just for Kids"

It's fun to go on a family vacation. And when you get old enough to take a train or plane ride on your own, it can be a special treat to visit relatives or family friends all by yourself.

No matter how exciting it is to travel, there are always times when it seems to take too long to get there. You have to sit still in an airport or the family car. Don't you wish you could run and jump, stretch your legs—or at least your imagination.

This book is meant for just these times. *The New England Guide and Activity Book for Young Travelers* puts your fingers and your mind to work. There are games and puzzles, stories to read, pictures to color—even your very own book to make.

You only need a few things to enjoy this book: a pencil with an eraser, some crayons, a roll of transparent tape, and a pair of scissors. There are several "How To" projects that require a few extras. But nothing that isn't easy to find—even when you are traveling.

This book has lots of different activities, because kids are not all the same. If you like to draw, you can use the blank "Scrapbook" pages for your own pictures. These pages also make good travel journals, if you would rather write about your trip. Or if you like to collect things, these pages are great for taping what you want to remind you of New England.

You may be surprised at how much you can learn—without even trying! There are maps of each state here and the United States, so you can always find where you are going. Read about the states you visit to see what makes New England a special place. There are also nature guides to help you recognize the different plants and animals you see here.

Don't forget the folks back home. Look for the postcards in this book (they are printed on heavy paper, so you can find them easily just by flipping through the book). You can color a picture, write a note, then carefully tear the card out to send to a friend.

Because you are doing and learning so much here in New England, you will want to make your very own badge or two. Look on page 91 to choose the badge that suits you best—maybe they all do! Just color, cut out, and tape a badge onto your shirt.

When you are ready to explore, this book can help you, too. There is a complete section, called "Places To Go" jam-packed with beaches, boat trips, hikes and nature walks, museums that are fun for kids, places to swim or fish, special events like fairs, maple sugaring, or whale watching. You will want to share this part of your book with your family. They will enjoy choosing where to go as much as you will.

USing A map

When you look at this map of the United States you can see that New England (the part that's shaded) is not very big. In fact, there are 21 states that are bigger than all 6 New England states put together.

Can you find the state you are from? Put an "X" in it.

Do you know how to read a map? First, make sure it is right side up. Just look for the compass and make sure the "N" is on top, or look for an arrow and make sure it is pointing upward. Once you know north is at the top, then EAST is always to the right, WEST is to the left, and SOUTH is at the bottom.

Fill in the blanks with NORTH, WEST, SOUTH, and EAST.

New England is _ _ _ _ _ _ and _ _ _ _ _ .

California is _ _ _ _ _ _ and _ _ _ _ _ .

The sun rises in the _ _ _ _ _ .

The sun sets in the _ _ _ _ _ .

Moss grows on the _ _ _ _ _ _ side of tree trunks.

In winter, it's warmer in the _ _ _ _ _ _ .

Most maps show you how far places are from each other. On this map of the 6 New England states, there is a scale which shows you how many miles equal 1 inch. Cut out the ruler on this page and use it to measure distances. How many inches is Boston, Massachusetts from Concord, New Hampshire? How many miles does that equal?

Which state is biggest? Which is smallest?

Color the states you have already visited in your favorite color.

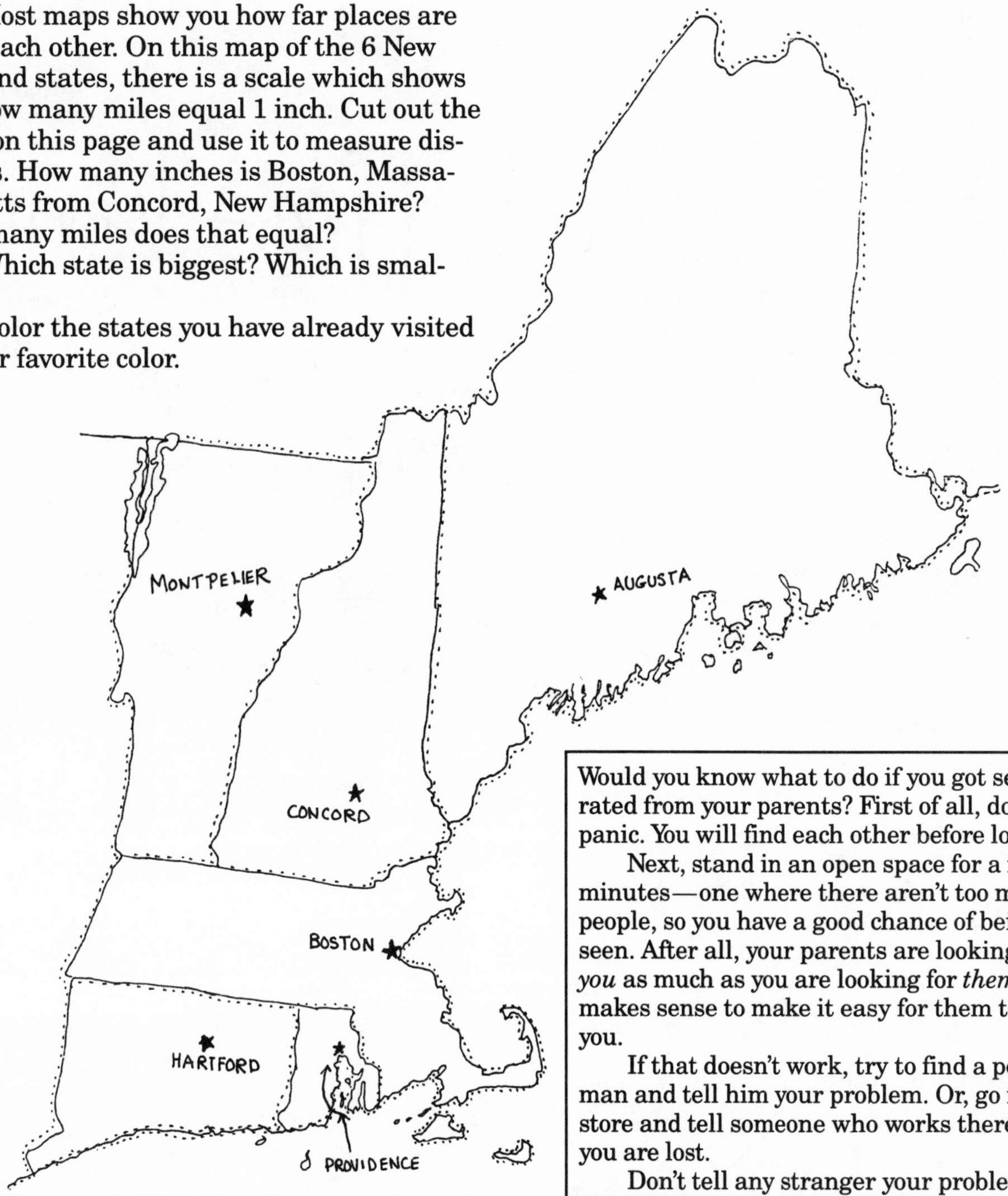

★ AUGUSTA

MONTPELIER ★

CONCORD ★

BOSTON ★

HARTFORD ★

δ PROVIDENCE

Would you know what to do if you got separated from your parents? First of all, don't panic. You will find each other before long.

Next, stand in an open space for a few minutes—one where there aren't too many people, so you have a good chance of being seen. After all, your parents are looking for *you* as much as you are looking for *them*. It makes sense to make it easy for them to find you.

If that doesn't work, try to find a policeman and tell him your problem. Or, go into a store and tell someone who works there that you are lost.

Don't tell any stranger your problem—only a policeman or someone who works in a store. They will help you find your parents. (It helps if you know what kind of car you came in, and the license plate number.)

The best thing to do is not get lost in the first place. That's easy if your family agrees to meet at a certain place if you do get separated.

80 mi.   160 mi.   240 mi.   320 mi.   400 mi.   480 mi.

inches   1   2   3   4   5   6

Lake Champlain is a warm, shallow sea 500,000,000

Appalachian and Green Mountains are formed 440,000,000

New England Time Line

Dragonflies appear 300,000,000

The Atlantic Ocean is born 200,000,000
Dinosaurs roam Connecticut; first birds appear 195,000,000

White Mountains are formed 150,000,000

Dinosaurs become extinct 130,000,000

First horseshoe crabs, frogs, scallops, and turtles appear 100,000,000

Whales swim in the Atlantic 30,000,000

Ice Age: glaciers cover New England; Cape Cod is formed 3,000,000

Last glaciers melt; low-lying areas are flooded 10,000
First human beings appear in New England 9,000
New England forests contain firs, oaks, pines, and spruces 7,500
New England Indians travel in dugout canoes and use fire . . . . 5,000 BC

1

New England uses clean, renewable energy? . . . . 2,0?? AD

New England Long Ago

You may be glad there are still dragonflies around, as you travel around New England. They eat mosquitoes!

Look at the time line on the opposite page. Read what happened here at different times.

Our world is very old. New England has changed a great deal over millions and millions of years. Where was the oldest sea?

What kinds of creatures have been around the longest?

Some animals, like dinosaurs and wooly mammoths, no longer exist. You can say they are extinct. Dinosaurs lived in New England for almost seventy million years (that looks like 70,000,000 in numerals—a lot of zeros.)

All that we know of extinct plants and animals comes from studying fossils. Fossils can be outlines imprinted in stone or they may be skeletons.

You can find fossils in museums all over New England. But there are fossils outdoors, too. Would you like to see the dinosaur footprints at Dinosaur State Park in Connecticut?

How long have there been pine trees in New England? Which has been here longer— the pine or the whale?

How much longer have dragonflies been around than people?

Look at the close-up of human history. We are a relatively new kind of animal, aren't we? People have lived on earth for only 11,000 years.

Many New Englanders are related to people who came here 300 years ago. Explorers from Europe began to sail across the Atlantic Ocean—no one really knew what lay ahead.

They found a rich land with tribes of Indians hunting and farming. Later, settlers from many different countries sailed to America. The English (later called the British) settlers came to the northeast coast. How do you think New England got its name? Many cities and towns here were named after places in England, too.

At first, the Indians welcomed these strange, pale-faced people from the boats without oars. In fact, if the native Americans hadn't showed them how to fish for lobsters or how to plant the hardy Indian corn, the settlers might not have stayed here at all.

Close-Up of Human History

Indians hunt, fish, and gather foods	5,000
Woodland Indians learn to farm, use calendars, begin earliest form of writing	3,000 BC
Vikings discover Martha's Vineyard	1,000 AD
England's John Cabot sails along NE coast	1,490
First American schoolbook is printed	1,689
Maine enters Union as free state	1,820
Connecticut elects first woman governor in US	1,974
Catamount Trail completed in Vermont	2,000
New England uses clean, renewable energy?	2,0??

Sensing New England

In these six states there are lots of things to see, hear, taste, touch, and smell. Many of them can be found only in this part of the country. Here's a checklist of things to be on the lookout for in New England. Put an "X" next to all the things you found here.

SEE

- ☐ Sap buckets on maple trees
- ☐ Waterwheel
- ☐ Windmill
- ☐ Gold dome
- ☐ Stone wall next to birch trees
- ☐ Widow's walk
- ☐ Moose
- ☐ Lobster boat
- ☐ Swan boat
- ☐ Lighthouse
- ☐ Pilgrim
- ☐ Covered bridge
- ☐ Ice fishing shack
- ☐ Indian
- ☐ Fish ladder
- ☐ Fort
- ☐ Round building
- ☐ Drawbridge
- ☐ Topiary
- ☐ Blueberry bush
- ☐ Rainbow
- ☐ Snow in July

TOUCH

- ☐ Cold ocean water
- ☐ Soft lake water
- ☐ Beach sand
- ☐ Cobblestone
- ☐ Granite
- ☐ Horseshoe crab
- ☐ Starfish
- ☐ Lichen
- ☐ Moss
- ☐ Morgan horse nose
- ☐ Lamb's ears

SMELL

- ☐ Low tide
- ☐ Pine woods
- ☐ Balsam bag
- ☐ Wild rose
- ☐ Skunk
- ☐ Skunk cabbage
- ☐ Herbs
- ☐ Salt air
- ☐ Peat bog
- ☐ Sugar shack
- ☐ Apple blossoms
- ☐ Mulled cider
- ☐ Jam kitchen
- ☐ Fish shanty

TASTE

- ☐ Boston baked beans
- ☐ Codfish cake
- ☐ Frappe
- ☐ Tonic
- ☐ Steamed hot dog
- ☐ Fried clam
- ☐ Maple sugar
- ☐ Lobster roll
- ☐ Cruller
- ☐ Boston cream pie
- ☐ Parker House roll
- ☐ Toll House cookie
- ☐ Tea from Tea Party ship
- ☐ Birch beer
- ☐ Moxie
- ☐ Strawberry shortcake
- ☐ Blueberry pie
- ☐ Beach plum jelly
- ☐ Apple cider

HEAR

- ☐ Seagull
- ☐ Fog horn
- ☐ Bell buoy
- ☐ Church bell ringing
- ☐ Peepers
- ☐ Bull frog
- ☐ Nighthawk
- ☐ Loon laughing
- ☐ Sailboat horn
- ☐ Somebody saying: "Ayuh"
- ☐ Somebody saying: "Pahk the cah"
- ☐ Somebody saying: "Bubbla"
- ☐ Steam train whistle
- ☐ Mosquito

CONNECTICUT

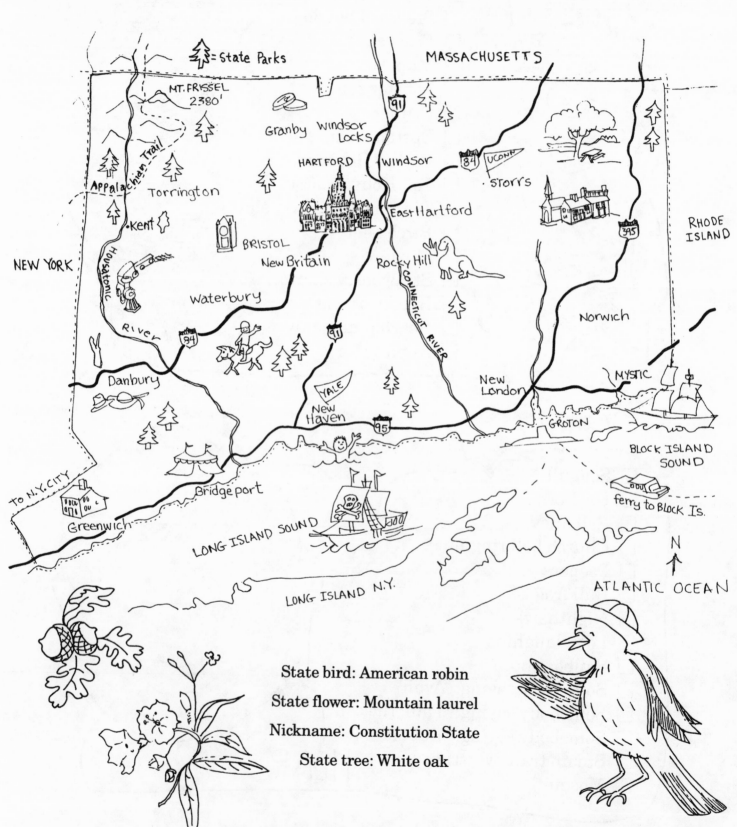

= State Parks

MASSACHUSETTS

MT. FRISSEL 2380'

Granby

Windsor Locks

HARTFORD

Windsor

UCONN

Storrs

Appalachian Trail

Torrington

East Hartford

RHODE ISLAND

NEW YORK

Kent

BRISTOL

New Britain

Rocky Hill

Housatonic

Waterbury

CONNECTICUT RIVER

River

84

91

Norwich

Danbury

YALE

New Haven

New London

MYSTIC

95

GROTON

BLOCK ISLAND SOUND

TO N.Y. CITY

Bridgeport

ferry to BLOCK Is.

Greenwich

LONG ISLAND SOUND

N

LONG ISLAND N.Y.

ATLANTIC OCEAN

State bird: American robin

State flower: Mountain laurel

Nickname: Constitution State

State tree: White oak

Connecticut is the southernmost New England state. More of its people live in cities than live in towns or the country. When you drive through this state on the interstates, you will see many factories and big office buildings. But you are never very far from woods or open space.

Wherever you go in Connecticut, you will be no more than a half-hour by car from a state park. Look at how many there are on the map! You can catch a fish, have a picnic, or take a swim in these parks. (Many are listed in "Places to Go" in the back of this book.)

You may be surprised to discover that most of this state is wooded. Near Cornwall, you can see huge pines that were growing when the first settlers came to New England. Or look at the old houses and ships Connecticut's people made from wood.

There are lots of activities that will help you learn about this state—and even more fun places to visit. But before you get started, you might enjoy reading some stories about Connecticut.

An Invitation Too Good to Refuse

Connecticut is the only part of New England where the Indians actually invited the English to come and settle. The peace-loving Connecticut tribes were afraid of more war-like Indians—the Pequots (say: PEE-kwats) and Mohawks. "The English will drive away these troublemakers with their hot-mouthed weapons," the peaceful Indians said. (What do you think "hot-mouthed weapons" were?)

Jack Straw, a Connecticut brave who spoke English, led his tribe to Plymouth. They offered the Pilgrims corn and furs, if they would settle along the Connecticut River. Slowly, settlers from Massachusetts began to venture into Connecticut.

> Did you know that Indians sold the land for one early settlement in Connecticut to the English for just 12 coats!

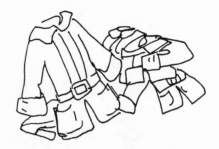

In England, the King's (or Queen's) word was law. In early New England settlements, people began to make laws themselves—since the King was so far away. But he still had to approve everything the colonists decided.

Religion was very important to the Massachusetts settlers. They decided that only church members could have any say in making laws. One Massachusetts settler, Thomas Hooker, moved to Connecticut because he felt this decision was not fair.

To Hooker, everyone who worked to clear land and build a community should have a say in making its laws—not just church members. In 1639, he and his followers were the first Americans to allow any free man to vote. (It would take women much longer to get the vote, but that is another story.)

Even the King of England put his seal of approval on Hooker's form of government—government *by* the people. The King signed a Royal Charter giving the Connecticut colonists the right to make all their own laws. And he let them decide what the punishment should be, if people broke these laws.

A charter is a written guarantee of rights and privileges *from* the ruler of a country *to* his people. The rules your parents set at home work a little like the laws and rights in a charter, except parents don't usually write them down.

Later, other English kings wanted more control over the colonies. England decided to make one man governor of all its settlements in America. When the new governor came to Connecticut, he wanted to change things.

How would you feel if your parents always let you decide what to wear, then left you with a sitter who said you could only wear one outfit? That's how the colonists felt when the new governor came to Connecticut.

In a meeting with colonial leaders, the governor asked to see the Royal Charter that gave Connecticut's people the right to govern themselves. Before the new governor could get his hands on the charter, all the candles in the room suddenly went out. By the time everyone could see again, the charter was gone!

One of the colonists, fearing the new governor might destroy it, had taken the charter away. He hid it in a hole in a large oak tree nearby.

You may notice the name Charter Oak if you visit Connecticut's capital, Hartford. The oak where the colonists' laws were hidden was struck by lightning some years ago, but people still remember how this tree saved their rights.

After the Revolution, the new American states tried to agree on a kind of government that would work for all of them. It was people from Connecticut who came up with an idea that most states liked. That's why Connecticut is called the Constitution State.

A constitution is like a charter because it lists people's rights and privileges. But most constitutions, like our American one, are written *by* the people *for* the people. Say your whole family gets together to settle an argument or plan a trip. When you come to an agreement, the decisions you reach together are a little like writing a constitution.

How many words can you make from Connecticut? From Constitution?

_____

_____

_____

_____

_____

_____

Connecticut the Dots and Color

This Star was born in Africa and joined Barnum's Circus in London.

He was the largest **ATHEPLEN** _____
(unscramble)
in the world!

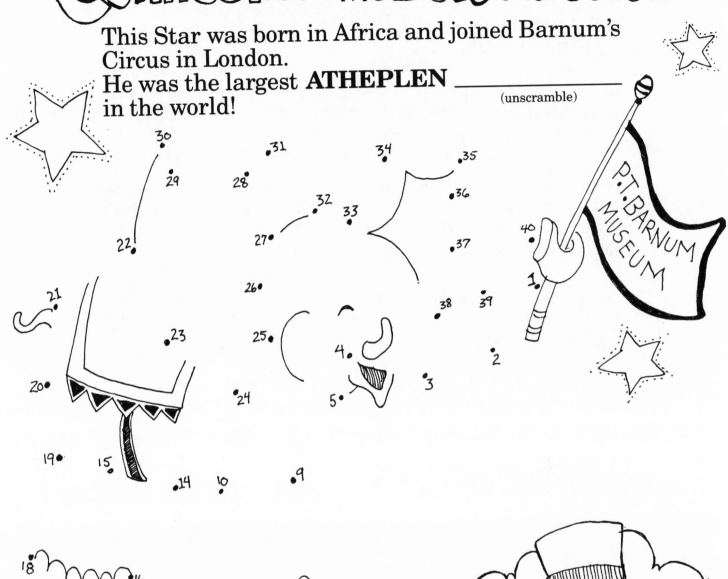

Other stars in the circus were "General" Tom Thumb, zebras, Zazel (a woman who was the first human cannonball), reindeer, a goat who rode a horse, and "Grizzly" Adams.

No wonder people called P.T. Barnum's Circus **"the Greatest Show on Earth!"**

If you visit the P.T. Barnum Museum in Bridgeport, Connecticut, you will see Tom Thumb's clothes. ("General" Thumb was a Midget.) Would his clothes fit you?

1 across)   In New Haven you can learn about plants and animals at the Peabody Museum of Natural History, part of __ a l __ University.

2 down)   Be sure to visit the _ _ _ _ _ s _ _ _ _ exhibit, where you will see specimens of huge reptiles that lived millions of years ago.

3 down)   Can you find the fossil of Brontosaurus (say: bron-tuh-Saw-russ) in this _ _ _ _ _ _ m? Brontosaurus means thunder lizard. How do you think this dinosaur got its name?

4 across)   Paintings on walls are called _ _ _ _ _ l s. The Age of Reptiles mural in Great Hall is 110 feet long. You can buy a poster of this mural at the museum shop, but you will need 6 feet of wall space to hang it.

5 down)   Brontosaurus had to eat a lot of plants to fill its huge _ _ _ _ _ a c h. How many heads of lettuce to you think this dinosaur could eat?

6 across)   Another dinosaur here in the museum is Deinonychus (say: Dine-ON-ee-cuss), which means "terrible claw." There are two _ _ _ _ _ _ t o n _   and one life-size model of this dinosaur in Great Hall.

7 down)   A museum is not the only place to find dinosaur _ _ _ s _ _ _ _ _ . At Dinosaur State Park in Rocky Hill, you will see footprints made by these huge reptiles. (Read the facing page to see how to make your own fossil cast.)

8 across)   When glaciers came, the _ _ o w and ice brought an end to the Age of Dinosaurs.

DINOSAURS

How to Make a Fossil Cast

At Dinosaur State Park, you can make casts of real fossils, or dinosaur footprints. You need to bring:

- one 10-pound bag of plaster of Paris
- 1/4 cup of cooking oil

The people at the park will give you everything else you need—and will help you make your cast.

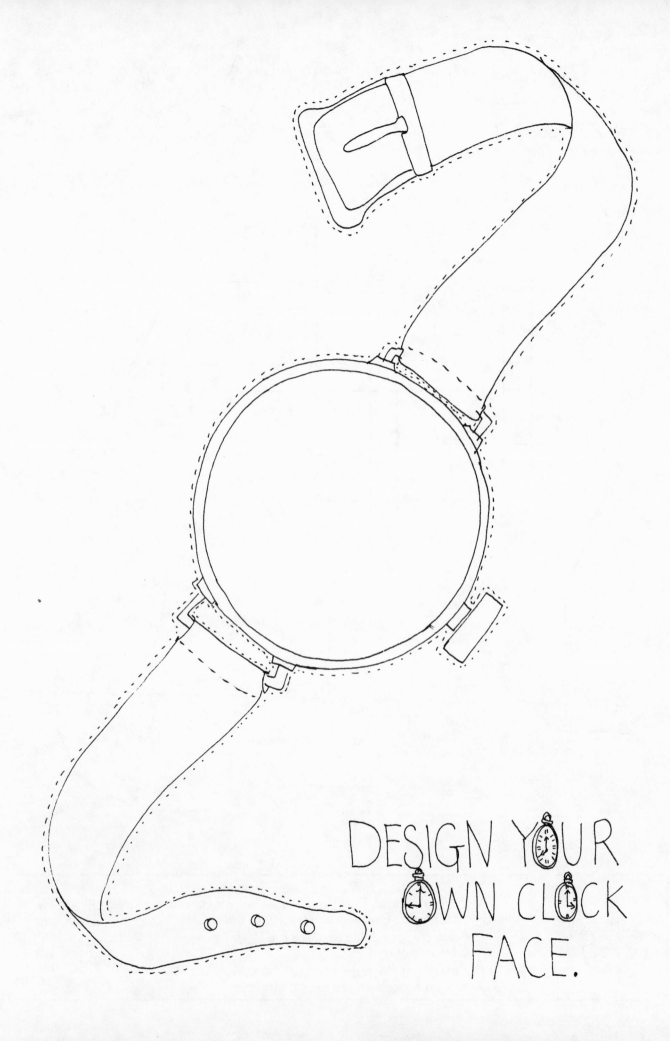

DESIGN YOUR
OWN CLOCK
FACE.

American Clock+Watch Museum

Eli Terry was a Connecticut inventor who came up with the idea that standard parts would fit in many different types of clocks. This made clocks cheaper to make and easier to fix. You can see some of Terry's clocks at the American Clock and Watch Museum, in Bristol. Yankee peddlers (salesmen from New England) sold clocks made in Connecticut throughout America.

Two different types of numbers are painted on clock faces to show the time.
Roman numerals look like this:

I II III IV V VI VII VIII IX X XI XII

Arabic numbers look like this:

1 2 3 4 5 6 7 8 9 10 11 12

Can you tell time on all these clocks? Find the clock that's missing its hands. Draw in hands to show what time you get up on school days.

What's wrong with two of the clocks?

Does a clock go "tick tock" or "tock tick"? Some clocks don't make any sound at all. Can you find two on this page?

Connecticut Yankees

Much of the soil in Connecticut is poor. Early on, colonists had to find another way, besides farming, to make a living. Some people became very good at making things. Boats, chairs, clocks, and toys from Connecticut were popular all over America.

Many items used in America were first invented or manufactured by someone from Connecticut.

Not all of us can invent things or work well with our hands. Some people are clever at selling—lots of people from Connecticut became good salesmen (and some still are).

Long ago, a Connecticut peddler would fill a wagon full of items made here, then travel up and down New England, selling thread or clocks or toys to people.

Made In Connecticut

Do you know why Connecticut is also called the "Nutmeg State?" Sometimes, its salesmen were not very honest. Some Connecticut peddlers would carve wood into the shape of the spice, nutmeg, and sell it. By the time a cook got around to shaving her "nutmeg" into the batter, the peddler would be long gone. And the buyer would be stuck with pancakes that tasted like sawdust!

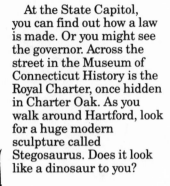

HARTFORD SIGHTSEEING

The Traveler's Tower is the tallest of Hartford's buildings—a good place to get a bird's eye view of the city.

In West Hartford, you can visit Noah Webster's home. He wrote a spelling book that became a best seller.

Who wrote *Huck Finn? A Connecticut Yankee In King Arthur's Court?* Mark Twain lived and wrote at Nook Farm.

At the State Capitol, you can find out how a law is made. Or you might see the governor. Across the street in the Museum of Connecticut History is the Royal Charter, once hidden in Charter Oak. As you walk around Hartford, look for a huge modern sculpture called Stegosaurus. Does it look like a dinosaur to you?

RED ROVER

In Bushnell Park, you can ride a merry-go-round, eat a hot dog, or listen to music right in the heart of the city.

The Old State House is a gift shop, museum, and visitor center—all in one! You can catch a double-decker bus here that will show you all the sights.

The Hartford area is a busy place. If you visit this part of Connecticut, draw a line from the bus to the places you actually saw. Color this picture.

Gillette Castle

High on a hilltop overlooking the Connecticut River is Gillette Castle, named for the actor who made Sherlock Holmes famous.

Sherlock Holmes was an English detective who wore a funny hat and smoked a pipe.

William Gillette lived in this castle with his favorite animals—cats. At one time he had 17. They're all hidden here. Can you find them?

CONNECTICUT
SCRAPBOOK

U.S.S. NAUTILUS

In Groton you can visit a submarine museum, called the Nautilus Memorial. It is on the Thames River (say: TEMS) next to the Submarine Base at New London.

The *Nautilus* is the world's first nuclear-powered sub. It could travel 60,000 miles on a lump of uranium no bigger than a golf ball. How many miles did you travel today?

In the museum building you can look through a periscope or pretend you're the captain in a real control room.

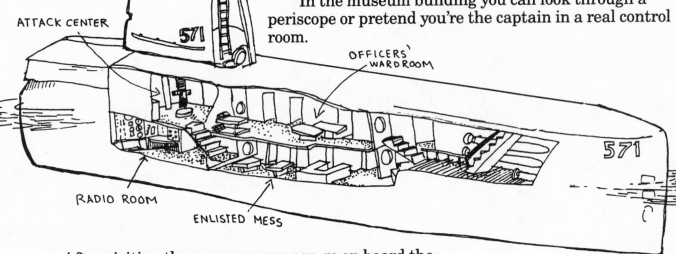

BRIDGE

ATTACK CENTER

571

OFFICERS' WARDROOM

RADIO ROOM

ENLISTED MESS

571

After visiting the museum, you can go on board the *Nautilus* and see what life would be like on a sub. Would you like to live under water for two months?

If you think you'd like to be a sailor in the "Silent Service" you will first have to train at the Submarine School in Groton.

Draw a line from each man to the place where he belongs.

EASY [2] DRAW SUBS

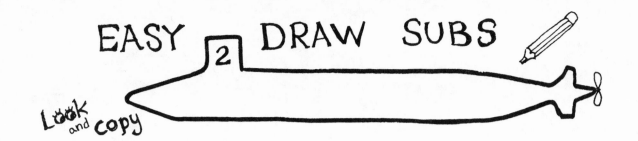

Look and copy

CREATE YOUR OWN SUBMARINE.

MAKE YOUR OWN PERISCOPE.

You need:
- long box (shoe box is good)
- 2 small mirrors
- tape
- scissors

③ Tape box top to bottom.

② Cut holes in the top (above where the mirrors are placed in the bottom)

① Tape the mirrors in a diagonal at each end of the box.

LOOK through the bottom hole. No one will be able to sneak up on you!

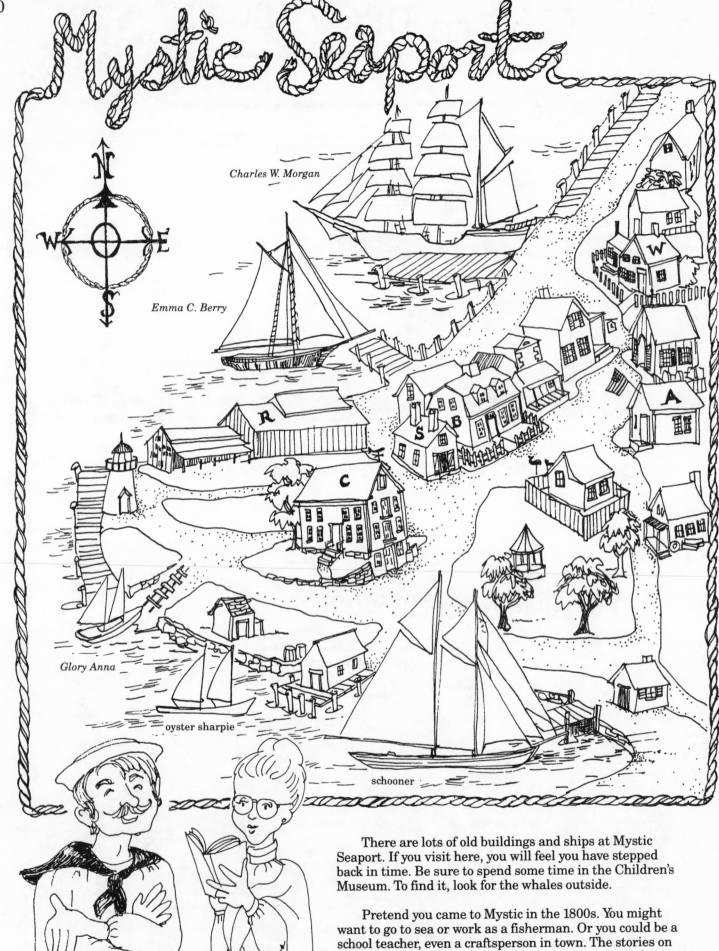

Mystic Seaport

Charles W. Morgan

Emma C. Berry

Glory Anna

oyster sharpie

schooner

There are lots of old buildings and ships at Mystic Seaport. If you visit here, you will feel you have stepped back in time. Be sure to spend some time in the Children's Museum. To find it, look for the whales outside.

Pretend you came to Mystic in the 1800s. You might want to go to sea or work as a fisherman. Or you could be a school teacher, even a craftsperson in town. The stories on the next page let you spend a day in someone else's shoes — just to see what it was like on the Mystic River long ago.

Pretend you are first mate on the *Charles W. Morgan*, a whaling ship. Your ship sails soon. Today you have things to buy for the voyage. Draw a line in green (or your favorite color) to show where you go on the facing page.

When the *Morgan* is not at sea, you live right in port (B). As much as you like to sail, you are glad to be at home with your family. (If you were captain of your own ship, you could take your family with you on long voyages.)

As you leave home to do your errands, check your money. The captain of the *Morgan* has given you $10 in paper money and three gold coins, each worth $2. How much do you have to spend?

First, go to the Ship's Chandlery (C) to buy a barrel of biscuits, called hardtack. One barrel costs $3. How much money do you have left?

Next, go up to the sail loft for some extra canvas. The sails on the *Morgan* would cover one-third of an acre (an acre is about the size of a football field). Sails carry your ship very far, very fast. If one is torn while you are at sea, it is important to be able to mend it quickly. (Do you see the sail loft above the Chandlery? Draw a circle around it.)

The whole floor of the sail loft is covered with canvas. You step carefully, trying not to tear any stitches. And you have to watch your head, too. The iron stove that warms the room hangs by chains from the ceiling, because there is no place for it on the floor.

The canvas costs $5. How much money do you have left?

Next, you walk over to the Shipsmith's (S) shop. You need some new cutting irons to remove blubber from the whales you hope to find. Each iron costs $2. You buy two of them.

Then you see a wonderful new kind of harpoon. You talk with the smith about it and decide you want that too. It costs $5. Do you have enough money left to buy the harpoon?

After you have what you need, take everything over to the *Morgan*. (Do you see this whaling ship on the map? Draw a circle around it.)

Suppose you were a young woman in Mystic. You might find work as a maid at the tavern, in a home "factory" like the weaving shop, or as a school teacher.

Pretend you are the teacher at the Boardman School. Draw a line in red (or another favorite color) to show where you would spend your day.

You leave your boarding house (W) early, so your students won't have to wait outside school (A) in the damp morning fog.

Before classes begin, two children bring in firewood to start the stove. But the schoolhouse stays chilly for a long time. You keep your shawl pulled tight across your shoulders for warmth.

There are only 17 students, but 5 grades. You ask the younger children to copy the alphabet on their slates. The older ones need to study Noah Webster's Blue-Backed Speller, before you test them.

You teach the 3 R's, history, and geography too. Both you and your students are busy all day long.

Two boys, who got into a fight at recess, stay late to wash off the blackboard and sweep up. You grade the spelling tests. Can you correct these words?

The sun is low in the sky as you lock up your school. Because the air is warm, you decide to take a walk before supper. Heading pass Chubb's Wharf and the *Morgan,* you see the *Emma C. Berry* coming in for the night. (Can you find this sloop on the opposite page? If so, draw a circle around it.)

As you pass the ropewalk (R), you notice a boy you taught last year. He is helping pull a braided cord almost as thick as his arm. The men and boys look like they are playing tug-of-war. The rope is very long and heavy. The ropewalk is the biggest building in port and employs the most people.

Cross the village green to go home. You see the lights of your boarding house. There is oyster stew to eat and you are hungry!

RHODE ISLAND

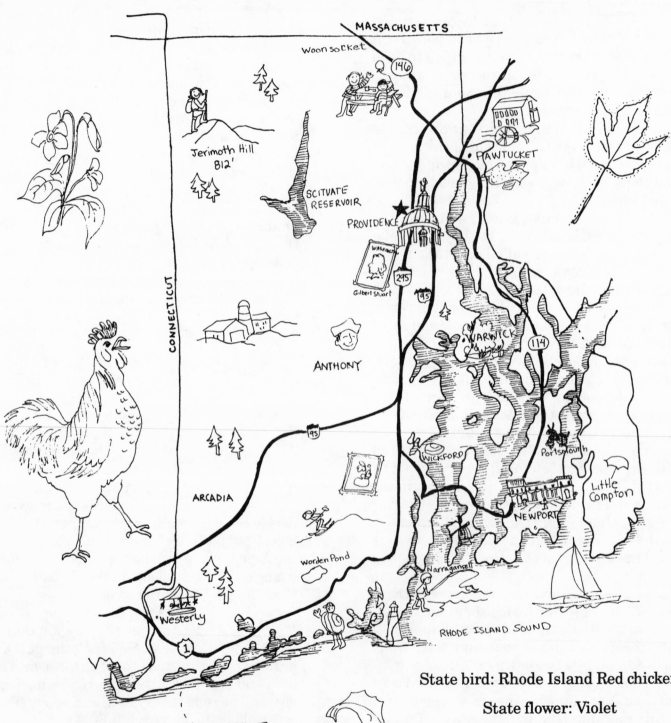

State bird: Rhode Island Red chicken

State flower: Violet

State tree: Red maple

Nickname: Ocean State

Do you know which state is the smallest? Rhode Island, of course! Most of its people live no more than 20 minutes from the capital, Providence.

If you drive into Rhode Island from Connecticut, you will probably be on Interstate 95. Say your car averages 60 miles per hour, and it takes one hour to get to Providence. How many miles did you go from the state border to the capital?

Providence wasn't always the capital. Four other places shared that honor: Newport, Bristol, South Kingstown, and East Greenwich. For a long time, Rhode Islanders were afraid of letting any one town have too much power in government. No wonder they put a statue of the Independent Man on top of their state house!

Rhode Island is a fun place to fish, swim, or sail a boat. You may see huge summer mansions, called "cottages," and bushes shaped like animals. There's a big wooden map of this state at the Children's Museum in Pawtucket—you can actually stand on it to move toy boats or trains around. This tiny state is a good place to have a New England clambake. Or try native American foods at an Indian restaurant, like the Dovecrest in Arcadia.

In Rhode Island, clams are called quahogs (say: KO-hogs). Look for the Grand Quahog in August at the Quahog Cook Off and Festival in Wickford.

What Cheer, Netop?

Roger Williams was Rhode Island's most famous settler. Roger was in trouble in Massachusetts. He didn't agree with the people who were running that colony. (They wanted everyone to worship God their way, and became very upset if people didn't follow the laws that church members made.) Roger refused to obey those laws, because he didn't think they were fair.

The court in Massachusetts wanted to punish him. But Roger had so many friends, the judges were afraid they would disobey, too. To keep others from following Roger's example, the judges decided to send him back to England.

A friend warned him of this plan. Because England allowed even less freedom than Massachusetts, Roger decided to start a new American settlement, where he could make his own rules. He had to leave home in a blizzard—just when his wife was expecting a baby.

He headed south for what is today Rhode Island. The first people he met here were Indians. Luckily, Roger had spent a long time learning Indian languages. When the braves greeted him with the words, "What Cheer, Netop?," he knew things would work out all right. (The Indian words meant "How're you doing, friend?")

When you visit Rhode Island, can you find any signs that remind you of those friendly words? Like "What Cheer Laundry" or "Netop Bottling Company"?

Roger and the Indians became good neighbors. Mrs. Williams, their children, and other people from Massachusetts soon arrived. Providence Plantation had begun. Roger called it that because he thought Providence (God) had provided very well for him.

Freedom for All

Unlike many settlers in America, Roger Williams was not looking for freedom just for himself. After all the trouble he had in England and Massachusetts, Roger felt it was only fair to allow everyone religious freedom. He let anyone who followed him to Rhode Island believe what she or he felt was right.

Rhode Island became known for its religious freedom. Driven out of Massachusetts for teaching about God, Anne Hutchinson followed Roger and started the town of Portsmouth. Quakers, who worship without ministers or priests, moved to Rhode Island (they were whipped and scorned in most other colonies). After they were turned away from New York, Jews from Europe settled in Newport.

Pretty soon, there was every kind of faith you can think of right here in this tiny colony. Today, you can see many different kinds of very old churches: Anglican (now called Episcopal), Baptist (Roger's church), Catholic, Congregational, Quaker, Unitarian, and the first Jewish synagogue ever built in the US.

The Ocean State

Because so many Rhode Islanders disagreed with other New Englanders, they turned away from the land and looked toward the sea. The state map will show you how easy it was for them to become sailors and shipbuilders.

Newport became the busiest seaport in New England. Shipbuilding got off to a good start here—and until recently, Rhode Island-built sailboats won every America's Cup Race.

Ships from this small colony circled the earth—but not always with honest cargo. Newport's Ted Tewes turned pirate. Do you see his own personal flag on page 27? Captain Kidd hid from the law in Narragansett Bay. His friend, Captain Paine, had a reputation as a pirate, too. Some people think Paine buried his treasure on Jamestown Island, but no one has found it—YET.

Many merchants in Newport made their fortunes in the Triangle Trade. Their ships carried molasses from the West Indies. Merchants turned molasses into rum in Rhode Island, then traded the rum for slaves in Africa. Finally, they sold the slaves in the West Indies, so they could buy more molasses.

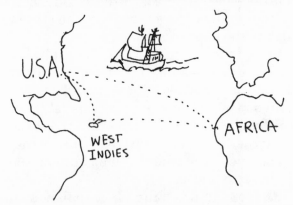

To be a slave meant that another person paid money to own you. Slavery had been around for thousands of years. Some of the Hebrews you read about in the Old Testament owned slaves; others were slaves. North American Indians had slaves, too.

In Africa, some tribes would capture young people of enemy tribes to sell as slaves. The first Africans were sold to Virginia colonists in 1619.

If you were a slave in America, it meant you had to work all day, every day, all your life for someone else. If a slaveowner was wise, he or she treated slaves well—seeing they had good food, a warm house, even a little education. But slaves remained *property,* unless their owner set them free.

In addition to slaves, prisoners and servants had to work very hard, too. But usually these people knew they would be free someday—after they had served their time or paid off their passage to America.

Many New Englanders earned a comfortable living in the Triangle Trade. Still more worked hard to end slavery in America.

Strange as it seems, this state whose people helped sell others was among the first to outlaw slavery within its boundaries. Even before the Revolution, there were free blacks holding respected jobs in Rhode Island. Newport Gardner started a music school here and gave lessons to his former owner. And the first regiment of black soldiers, who fought bravely in the American Revolution, came from Rhode Island.

If you visit Westerly, you can ride on a flying horse carousel at Watch Hill. This is not an ordinary merry-go-round with animals that slide up and down poles. These animals are suspended from the ceiling and swing outwards, as the carousel moves faster and faster. Nobody knows how the carousel got to Watch Hill. But some people think it was left behind when gypsies from a traveling circus ran out of money and left town.

the *Flying Horses of Watch Hill*

What are the differences between these two pictures?

RHODE ISLAND SCRAPBOOK

'X' Marks the Spot

These directions to a pirate's hidden treasure were in a bottle that washed up on the beach. You will have to use all your senses to find the treasure. Follow the directions carefully, and mark an X where you think the chest is buried. (**HINT:** Mark your path with arrows, so you don't lose your direction.)

1) Start in the LOWER RIGHT-HAND CORNER. 2) Go WEST. 3) When you bump into something made of wood, turn RIGHT. 4) If you step on acorns, turn EAST. 5) When your feet get wet, go NORTH. 6) If you hear a seagull, go WEST. 7) When you bump into rocks, turn RIGHT. 8) If you hear running water, turn around completely two times and head EAST. 9) When you smell pine trees, go STRAIGHT AHEAD. 10) If you hear bats, turn around and HEAD WEST. 11) After you hear branches creaking in the wind, TURN RIGHT. 12) The treasure is straight ahead, under something that smells sweet.

ALPHABET FLAGS

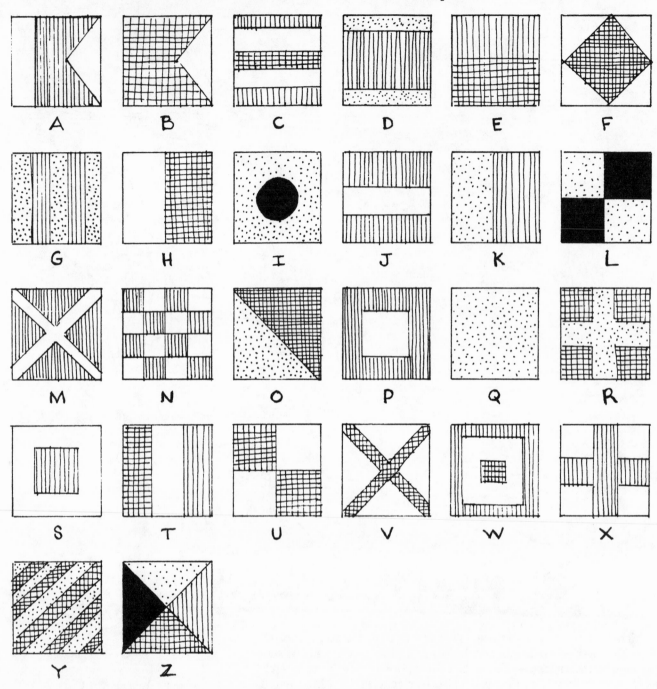

Sailboats and yachts from around the world navigate Newport's waters. The captains all speak the same language—the language of flags. Color the flags above to learn the letters in this international sailing alphabet. Then read the message a ship has signaled to you on the next page.

WHITE YELLOW RED BLUE BLACK

29

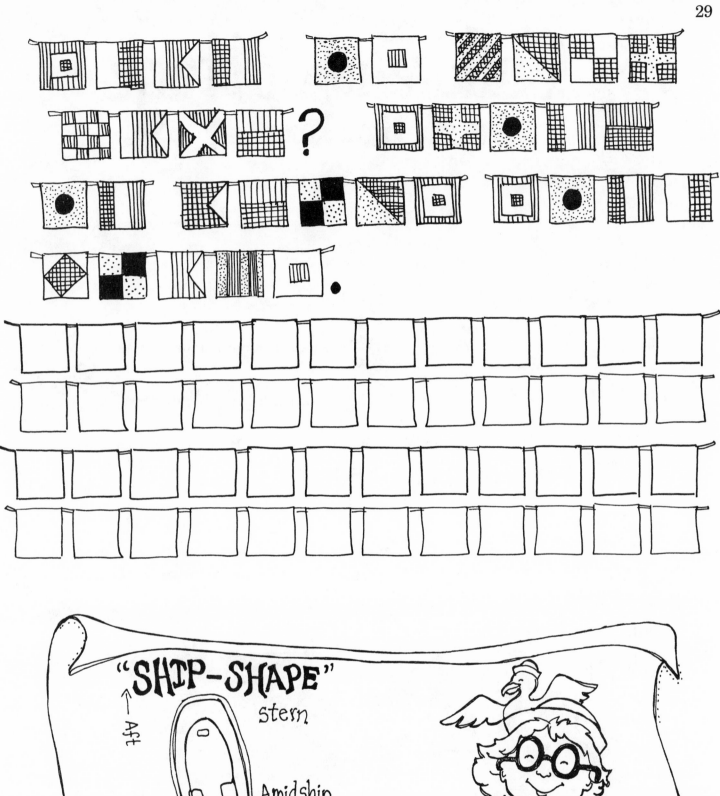

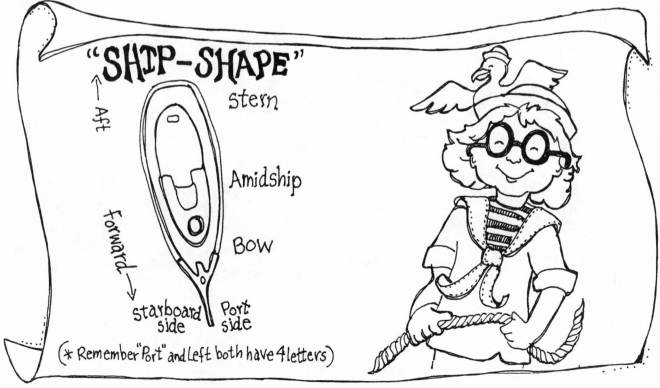

"SHIP-SHAPE"

Aft →

stern

Amidship

Bow

forward →

starboard side   Port side

(* Remember "Port" and Left both have 4 letters)

THE Children's Cottage
AT THE Breakers

1 down) Newport has been called the playground of the _ _ _ _ h.

2 across) The huge houses along the shore are called

c o t _ _ _ _ _ _ _ .

3 down) If you take the Cliff W _ _ _ _ , you can see many of these elegant mansions or "cottages."

4 across) The Astors and the Vanderbilts were _ _ _ _ _ _ b o r s in Newport.

5 across) When Mrs. Astor had a dinner party with 100 guests, there would be 100 s e r _ _ _ _ _ _ — one for each guest.

6 down) But even the Astors found it hard to outdo the _ _ _ n d _ _ _ _ _ _ s next door.

7 across) The Vanderbilt girls had their very own cottage — the size of most people's homes — for their _ _ _ _ parties.

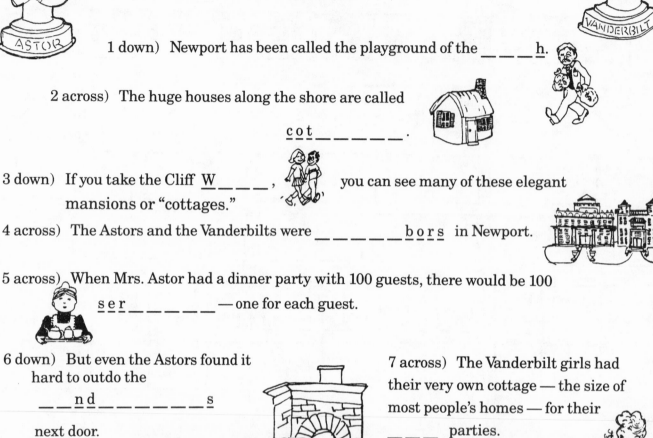

GREEN ANIMALS

In Portsmouth you can visit a wonderful garden called Green Animals. Trees and bushes shaped like animals are called topiary (say TOPE-ee-ar-ee).

Can you find a giraffe, an elephant, and a camel hidden in this picture? Each letter of the word T-O-P-I-A-R-Y is in the picture and stands for a different color. Choose seven of your favorite colors. Then fill in all the spaces that have the same letter with the same color.

At Green Animals, you can see lots of other trees shaped like animals—even one that looks like a policeman, and one in the shape of a sailboat.

Near the topiary garden is a children's museum with toy soldiers, dolls, and model cars, boats, trains, and planes.

Slater Mill Historic Site

In Pawtucket, you can visit the first cotton mill in America. It was built by Samuel Slater, who designed it entirely from plans he had memorized when he lived in England.

Look very closely at the clothes you are wearing. Can you see how the threads cross each other? They were woven together on a loom at a mill.

The cotton was made into threads of yarn and spun around spindles. When the spindles were full, they were taken to a different mill, where the yarn was woven into cloth.

Years ago, mills were built next to rivers, where the flowing water could be used to turn the wheels that spun yarn. As you travel throughout New England, you will see many mills along the rivers.

Color all the wheels you see in this picture red. How many did you find?

Massachusetts is not a big state—even for New England. In fact, you could fit 19 states the size of Massachusetts into California. But you don't have to be big to be important!

The Pilgrims landed in Massachusetts in 1620 and started the first English colony in New England. Other parts of New England were settled by people from Massachusetts. The Revolutionary War began in this small state. You could say that the United States would not be a country, if it weren't for Massachusetts.

Some of America's most important people came from Massachusetts, including presidents John Adams, John Quincy Adams, and John F. Kennedy.

Do you know about the famous Mr. and Mrs. Mallard from the story, *Make Way for Ducklings*? They—and their eight children—lived in the Boston Public Garden. Do you remember their names? Jack, Kack, Lack, Mack, Nack, Ouack, Pack, and Quack. Be sure to take a swan boat ride when you visit Boston.

If you visit Boston in the summertime, you can watch a baseball game at Fenway Park. Do you know the name of the home team? (Hint: part of the name is a color; the other part sounds like something you wear on your feet.)

Where else would you go if you were visiting Massachusetts? How about the sandy beaches of Cape Cod? Or Plymouth or Sturbridge where the past seems to come alive again. Maybe the huge cotton mills in Lowell?

Massachusetts is known as the "Bay State" because there are so many bays along the Atlantic Ocean. A bay is a small part of the sea set off by a piece of land. Look on the map to see how Cape Cod forms a bay. Massachusetts could also be called the "Beach State" because there are so many places to swim.

CAPE COD BAY

Away from the ocean, the land in Massachusetts is gently rolling, with lots of rivers, ponds, forests, farms, and small towns. There are even some low mountains in the western end of the state—the part next to New York.

There are big cities, too, like Worcester (say: WUS-tuh) and Springfield—and of course, Boston.

Massachusetts looks a lot different than it did when the Pilgrims arrived in 1620, but some things never change. As you travel through this state, look for things that might have looked the same to the first settlers. If you would like to know more about the Pilgrims, turn to page 44.

Do you know about the American Revolution?

While the first settlers in Massachusetts came from England, people born here thought of themselves as Bay Colonists or Americans. By the 1700s, many Massachusetts colonists had never been to England.

The Massachusetts Colony prospered. John Adams went to an American college (Harvard). Paul Revere made things, like silver tea pots, that Americans needed and liked. Because the Mother Country was so far away, the colonists got used to providing what they needed—whether it was writing laws or making their own clothes.

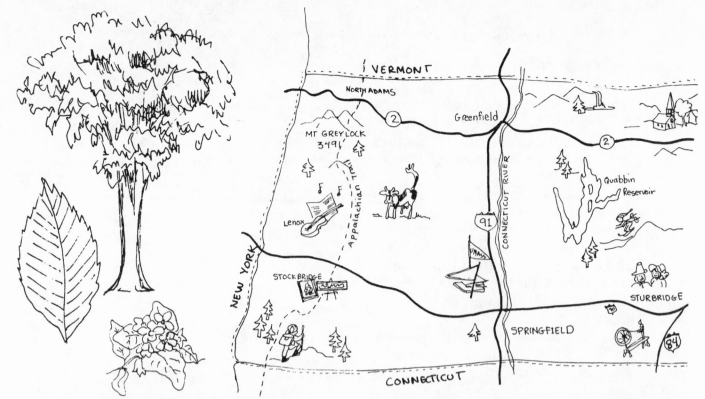

But Britain had many colonies and a plan for each of them. Unfortunately, the British plan didn't always fit what the colonists needed.

In Massachusetts, the colonists became angry when the British expected them to pay taxes on things they wanted to buy from England—especially when these were the same items the Mother Country didn't let them make in America. For the colonists, it made a lot more sense to trade among themselves than to follow the rules Britain laid down. What would you do if you were a colonist in Massachusetts and felt Britain's taxes were unfair?

The first thing the colonists did was complain to the King of England. When that didn't work, they decided to stop buying things from England. That made the British mad, because they would lose money if they couldn't sell their goods to the colonists.

The British responded by taking away more privileges from the colonists. Many people in Boston began to riot, so the British sent soldiers there. During one riot in 1770, known as the Boston Massacre, British troops fired on unarmed Americans. Several Bostonians were killed.

Over the next three years, things got worse. When the British made the colonists pay a tax on tea, 50 colonists dressed up as Indians boarded a ship loaded with tea chests and dumped 45 tons of tea into Boston Harbor. This was called the Boston Tea Party. (If you go to Boston, be sure to visit the Tea Party Ship, which looks just like the one from 1773. People on board will tell you all about what happened.)

Things got worse and worse for the next two years, until finally on April 19, 1775 war between the colonists and Britain broke out in Concord, Massachusetts with the "shot heard 'round the world." Farmers from up and down New England had been gathering weapons and gunpowder. When the patriots from Massachusetts called for help, colonists from all over New England joined in the fight.

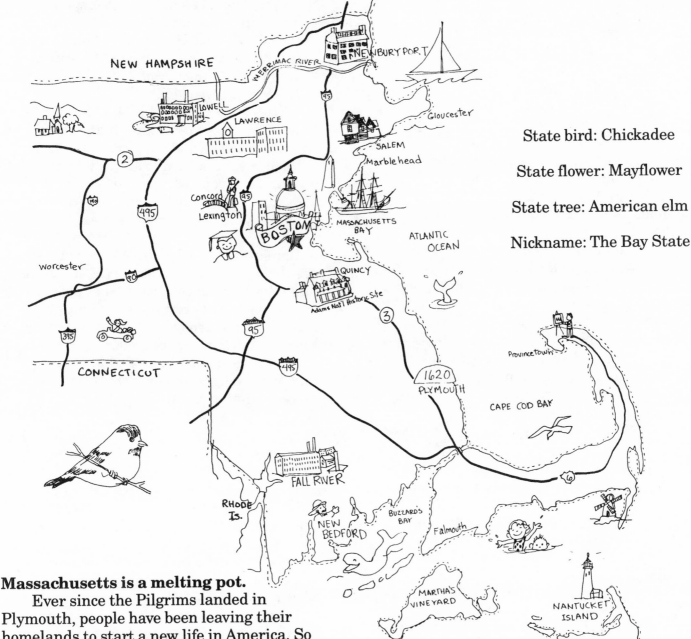

State bird: Chickadee

State flower: Mayflower

State tree: American elm

Nickname: The Bay State

Massachusetts is a melting pot.

Ever since the Pilgrims landed in Plymouth, people have been leaving their homelands to start a new life in America. So many of them moved to Massachusetts that it is often called a melting pot.

When you put some marshmallows, a block of chocolate, and some peanut butter in a pot on the stove and turn on the heat, they all melt and become mixed together. That's what has happened with people in America, but especially in the cities and towns of Massachusetts. People from Canada, Ireland, Italy, Germany, Scotland, and Poland blend together as Bay Staters.

Many people of Irish and Italian descent live in Boston. Those from Portugal settled in New Bedford and Gloucester (say: GLOSS-tuh). And Canadians live in the mill cities of Lowell and Lawrence. What nationality are the names O'Grady, Murphy, and Kennedy? How about Manicotti, Pepperoni, and Fetuccine?

Massachusetts people like to celebrate their foreign ancestry with festivals. In Boston's North End, you can join in the Italian Feasts every summer weekend. In Gloucester or New Bedford you can watch the Portuguese custom of the Blessing of the Fleet. Or celebrate with the Polish at the World Kielbasa (say keel-BAH-sah) Festival. There is even an Indian Pow-Wow on Cape Cod.

What country is your family from originally? Your name may be O'Shaughnessy or Stravinsky, but if you were born in the United States, you are an American. If you are visiting Massachusetts from a foreign country, you will have plenty of company. Welcome to the melting pot!

Watching Whales

At New Bedford's Whaling Museum, you can learn how dangerous it was for sailors in rowboats and wooden ships to hunt whales. Look for the skeleton of a humpback whale. Compare that to a whale boat. Which is bigger?

Your family might also enjoy a whale watch—a boat trip that looks for whales and tells you many interesting facts about them. Circle any of the whales on the next page that you see. (Hint: One can be found in the Mystic Marineland Aquarium in Connecticut.)

Whales look like huge fish. But they are really mammals that live in the ocean.

Whales have lungs, and they breathe through blow-holes in their heads, not through their mouths. A whale can hold its breath for as long as an hour. Then it comes up to the surface of the sea to blow out air from its giant lungs. And it inhales fresh oxygen before it dives again.

Whales also have skin, rather than scales like fish. Unlike many other mammals who live where it's cold, whales have no fur (only a little hair that is hard to see). Blubber, a thick layer of fat, keeps whales warm in icy water. This fat also prevents them from starving when they can't find enough to eat.

Like many fish, whales have eyes on either side of their heads. You won't be able to see their ears, but whales can hear sounds and vibrations in the water. They seem to sing to each other or talk by making clicking sounds. Whales may be as smart as we are—without having to go to school!

There are two kinds of whales: baleen and toothed. If you go on a whale watch, look at each whale's mouth.

Baleen Whales

If a whale looks like it has a moustache, it is a baleen whale.

A baleen whale has horny strips that hang from the roof of its mouth. Baleen works like a filter. These whales swim with their mouths open, letting in sea water full of food. Once the whales have a good "catch," they can close their mouths, squirting sea water back out through their baleen without giving up any "dinner."

The minke whale is a small baleen whale—if 6 to 8 tons is small! Look for a white patch on its flippers.

Sometimes a New England whale watch is lucky enough to spot a right whale.

There are only 300 right whales left in the whole world! Aren't you glad Massachusetts is working to protect these whales?

Humpback whales have black backs with white throats and bellies. They can go for months without eating, and like to feed in New England waters. They dive together, then swim upward blowing out bubbles. Watch for their "bubble nets," when you see these whales. Some people think humpbacks use these "nets" to catch the tiny fish they eat.

Toothed Whales

Toothed whales have fatty bumps on their heads (called melons), only one blowhole, and sharp teeth.

Whales don't need many teeth. Some have only two. Others have 50 teeth. Count the teeth on the picture of the sperm whale. How many do you see?

Sperm whales are the biggest toothed whales, measuring up to 60 feet long.

The sperm whale is the symbol of the Hartford Whalers hockey team.

Killer whales get their name because they will attack even bigger whales. Working together in a pack, they eat almost anything: birds, fish, porpoises, seals, or walruses. Sometimes called orca, a killer whale is easy to spot, because it has a 6 foot fin on its back. It is also black and white with a spot over its eye.

Beluga whales make whistling sounds when they talk—as well as burps, chirps, croaks, mews, moos, squeaks, and screams. Gray at birth, these Arctic whales turn white when they mature.

_____
pamhbuck

Look How Big Whales Are!

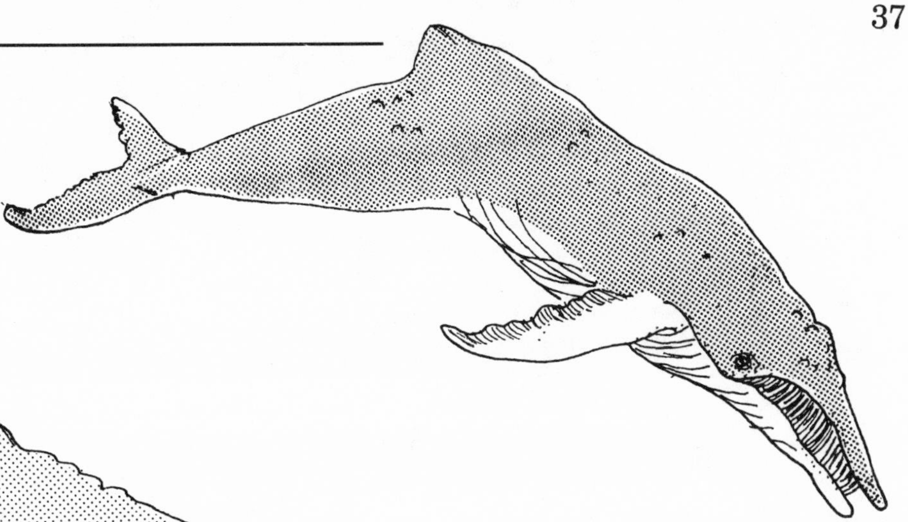

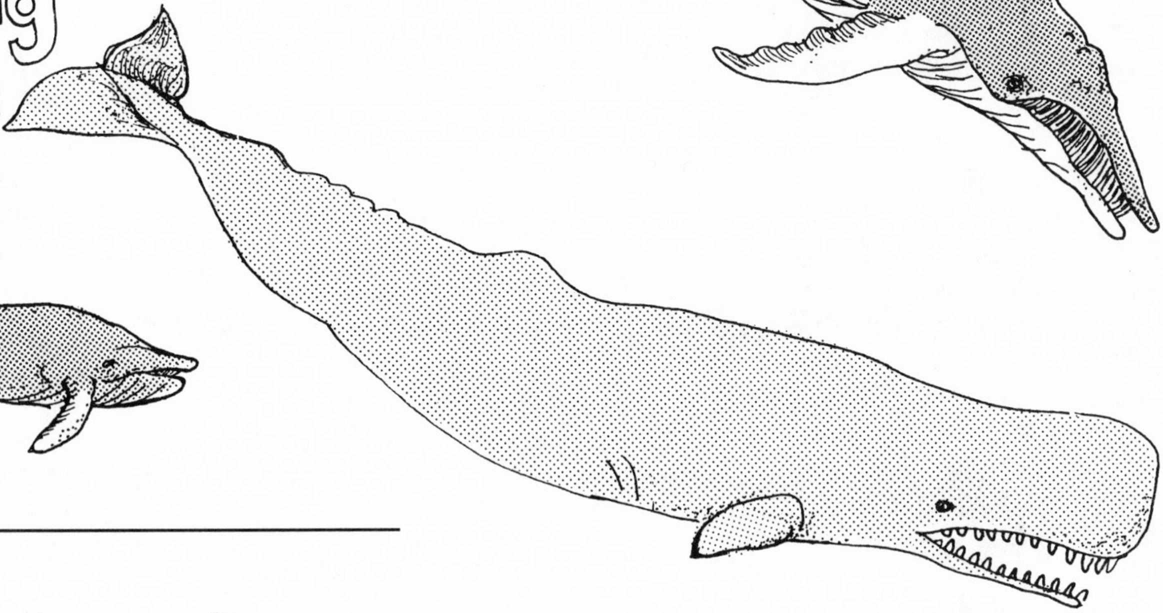

_____
kinme hawle

_____
prems elahw

Connecticut's state mammal

_____
lerkil ahelw

Massachusetts' state mammal

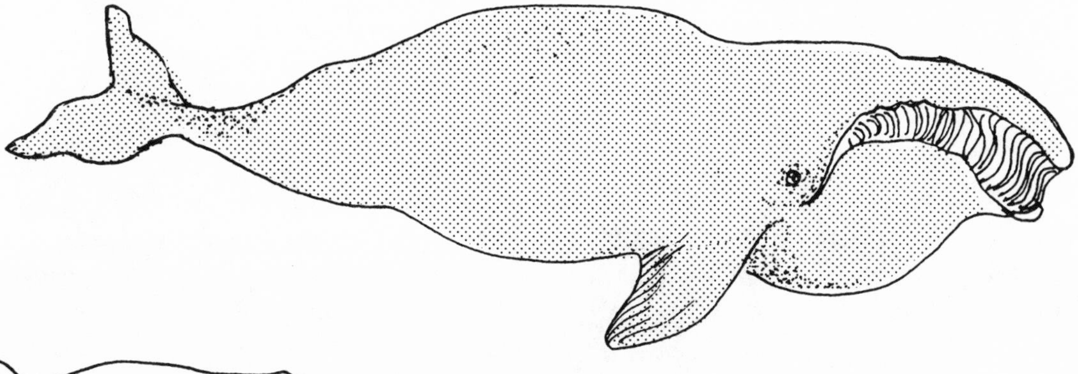

_____
grith laweh

_____
alubge

CAPE COD NATURE HUNT

Color all the plants and animals you have seen on Cape Cod.

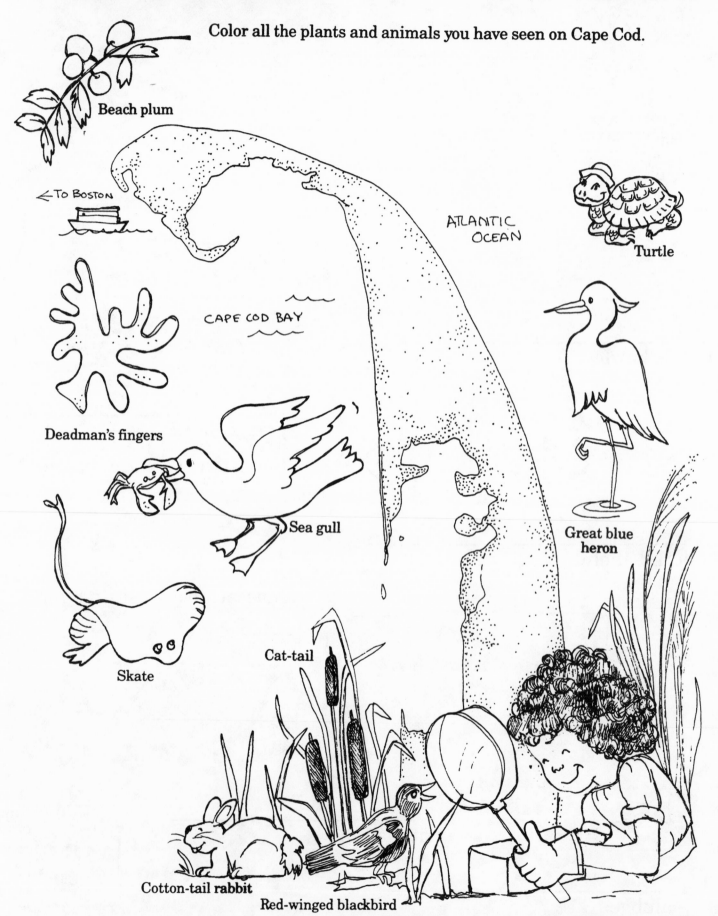

Beach plum

←TO BOSTON

ATLANTIC OCEAN

Turtle

CAPE COD BAY

Deadman's fingers

Sea gull

Great blue heron

Skate

Cat-tail

Cotton-tail rabbit

Red-winged blackbird

Rose

Canada Goose

Mermaid's purse

Woodpecker

Horseshoe crab

Sea Cucumber

Tern

Duck

Starfish

Clam

Fiddler crab

Dragon fly

Butterfly

Greenhead fly

Squirrel

Frog

If you colored more than 10, you are a true naturalist!

Poison Ivy

The Thornton Burgess Museum

THE CROOKED LITTLE PATH

A Book of Nature Stories *by* THORNTON W. BURGESS

Illustrated by HARRISON CADY

When you visit here you will see many books written by Thornton W. Burgess and illustrated by Harrison Cady. Here are some of their animal friends.

Reddy Fox

Bobby Coon

Little Joe Otter

Buster Bear

Mrs. Peter

Make your Own Book!

① Cut along the dotted lines.

② Fold at 1st fold line.

③ Open. Fold at 2nd fold line.

④ Holding each end, push inward.

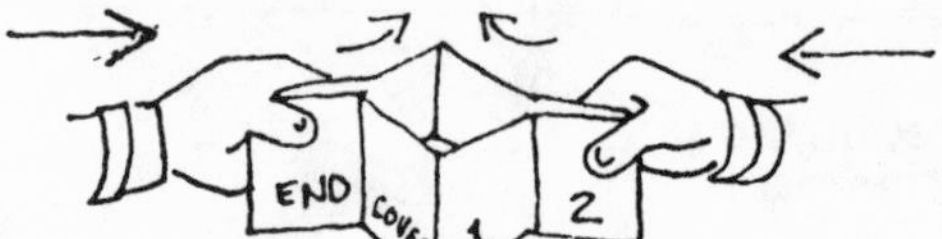

⑤ Pinch together, so front and back covers enclose the pages.

(Trace over dots.)

Peter Rabbit's Friends

⑥ Crease the edge. Fill in the blanks and color!

Hooray for You!

Make your Own Book!

(2nd fold)

and

2.

Then he met

3.

Peter Rabbit
met his friends

1.

(1st fold)

(1st fold)

and

4.

Together they
walked to the
Briar Patch to pick

5.

Peter Rabbit's
Friends

FRONT COVER

who made a
for her friends.

6.

They gave the black-
berries to

THE
END

(2nd fold)

Inspired by Thorton Burgess
and Harrison Cady and

(your name)

BACK COVER

CATCH the FERRY

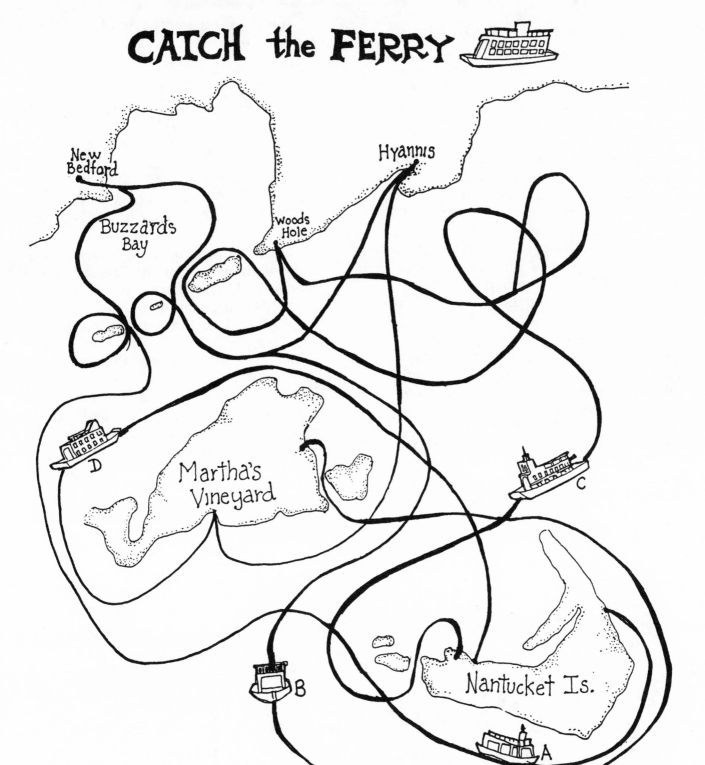

Ferries A, B, C, and D go between the mainland of Massachusetts and the islands of Martha's Vineyard and Nantucket. Can you figure out which ferry goes where? Look at the maze, and then put the correct letters in the spaces below:

1. Ferry ____ leaves Woods Hole and arrives at Nantucket Island.
2. Ferry ____ leaves New Bedford and arrives at Martha's Vineyard.
3. Ferry ____ leaves Hyannis and stops at Martha's Vineyard on the way to Nantucket Island.
4. Ferry ____ leaves New Bedford and arrives at Nantucket Island.

44 Saints + Strangers = The Pilgrims

In England, there was only one church. If you didn't agree with what its priests said or if you wanted to worship God in another way, you broke the law. Some people felt this was wrong. Because they risked their lives for their beliefs, they were called Saints.

Many Saints left England. They landed in Holland first, where they lived for twelve years, but they were afraid their children would lose their English ways. Some Saints began to think about the New World.

It cost a great deal of money to travel across the ocean. It cost even more money to start a new settlement. A group of English merchants offered the Saints a chance to leave Holland for America. The merchants would hire a ship and crew. They promised to buy all the food, tools, and supplies the Saints needed. But the Saints would have to promise to work for seven years to pay back the merchants. 35 agreed to go.

Because not all the Saints wanted to leave, the merchants needed more people to start a colony. They talked with some poor people, who wanted a chance to start a new life in a new country. Because they did not know each other or the Saints, they were known as Strangers.

It was easy to tell the Saints and the Strangers apart:

Saints wore simple, dark-colored clothes. While often poor, Strangers dressed in bright colors—with a bit of braid, pretty buttons, lace, ribbon, even feathers.

Because both Saints and Strangers had to make a long, difficult voyage to America, we remember them both as Pilgrims, or travelers.

Did you know that the Pilgrims had two ships? One was the *Mayflower*, and the other was the *Speedwell*. But the *Speedwell* was so leaky that it was left behind in England.

The *Mayflower* was not a passenger ship. It usually carried wine. The Pilgrims had to clean and scrub it before they could use it. They were lucky it didn't carry fish!

MAKE YOUR OWN "MAYFLOWER"

You will need: WALNUT, GUM or WAX, TOOTHPICKS, PAPER, SCISSORS

① Crack walnut in half saving the best half. (Eat the inside)

② Soften gum or wax and put in shell. Let it harden.

③ Cut sail from paper.

④ Stick toothpick through paper.

⑤ Stick toothpick and sail in the wax or gum in shell.

Float on Water. "SAIL ON"

The *Mayflower* was not very comfortable. It had no toilets, and the only beds were in the captain's quarters. When the *Speedwell* was left behind, the *Mayflower* became very crowded. Every inch of space was filled, usually with someone trying to sleep. Many people had to sleep on blankets on the deck floors—even though the fall air was very chilly and the seas were often rough.

Two babies were born at sea. In all, there were 33 children on board the *Mayflower*. Do you think they had fun?

The Pilgrim children could play on deck. Going across the ocean then was as exciting and dangerous as traveling in space today. But they had to eat cold food—salted fish or meat, cheese, hard biscuits. No one could take a bath (maybe you would like that).

In one storm, the *Mayflower* was blown off course. One man was swept overboard. But he was able to hold on to a rope, until the crew could save him.

If you visit Plymouth, you can see the *Mayflower II*. It looks just like the ship the Pilgrims sailed in. Would you like to spend 66 days crossing the Atlantic Ocean in a ship like this?

In November, over two months after the *Mayflower* left England, the crew finally sighted land. The Pilgrims fell to their knees. They thanked God for a safe voyage.

The Saints and the Strangers agreed to work together. They decided to elect a governor, and all promised to obey him. The agreement they signed is called the Mayflower Compact. The men voted—something they had not been allowed to do in England.

A group of men sailed off in a small boat to see if this was a good place to settle. When they returned to the *Mayflower*, the explorers said they found only "wilderness, full of wild beasts and wild men." But they made one important discovery—they found strange seeds of many colors planted in mounds under the soil. That seed—corn seed—would grow enough food to feed the whole colony.

The Pilgrims explored some more, until they found a safe harbor. They found woods filled with deer, wild fowl, and rabbits. There were nuts and berries, even sassafras, with root bark to use as medicine.

Plymouth

The settlers named their new home after the city they had left in England. On Christmas day, they began building a large house where all could keep warm. It was hard work because the ground was frozen and they were cold.

Many people got sick. Less than half the settlers lived through that first winter at Plymouth.

In spring, the *Mayflower* sailed back to England. it must have been very hard not to return to their homes, but the Pilgrims were determined to make a better life for themselves in America.

The settlers cut down trees to clear land for farming. They planted the seeds they had brought from home and the Indian corn. They built more houses and a fence around Plymouth. Captain Miles Standish trained the men to shoot straight, in case Indians attacked.

Luckily, the settlers met friendly Indians. Squanto spoke English. He taught the settlers how to plant corn and showed them how to make the soil rich. He told the settlers not to plant until the oak leaves were the size of mouse ears. Without Squanto, the settlers would not have learned to fish through winter's ice or to catch eels by hand in warm weather.

They made an agreement to live in peace with the Indians. To celebrate their first harvest, the Pilgrims invited their new friends to join them for a feast.

46

1. The "T"
2. Fenway Park
3. Public Garden
4. State House
5. Custom House
6. Beacon Hill
7. Charles River
8. Trinity Church
9. Boston Garden
10. Kennedy Library
11. Quincy Market
12. Faneuil Hall
13. Chinatown

BOSTON SIGHTSEEING

14. Bunker Hill Monument
15. USS Constitution
16. Park Street Church
17. New England Aquarium
18. Southeast Expressway
19. Old North Church
20. Old State House
21. Museum of Science

Match the places with the clues. Put the correct numbers from the opposite page in the boxes below.

☐ "Old Ironsides."
☐ Watch out for the sharks.
☐ "One if by land, two if by sea."
☐ Home of the Red Sox.
☐ Where Mr. & Mrs. Mallard & family live.

☐ It has a gold dome.
☐ You can see stars in the daytime here.
☐ Home of the Bruins & Celtics.
☐ This goes underground.
☐ There's a grasshopper on top.

Lexington

Minutemen were New England colonists who fought for their liberty at Lexington and Concord on April 19, 1775—the first battles of the Revolutionary War. The name "Minutemen" means they promised to be ready in a minute—if called to war. Most of them were farmers (not soldiers), but many of them had fought one-on-one with the Indians. All knew how to use their rifles from hunting wild game.

Some of the Minutemen's wives also fought in the Revolutionary War. They defended their homes and families while their husbands were away.

Concord

The British Redcoats did not expect to greet nearly 4,000 Minutemen in Lexington, Concord, and other towns along the route from
Boston. Paul Revere and William Dawes had warned the colonists
that the British were coming. The Redcoats lost the first battles of the
American Revolution—and hurried back to safety in Boston.

Sturbridge Village looks like any New England town in the 1830s. If you visit here, you will learn a lot about the past. What doesn't belong in this old-fashioned village?

What Is Out of Place in Sturbridge Village?

In the summer, the famous Boston Symphony Orchestra moves to the cool Berkshire Mountains to practice.

If you happen to be near the town of Lenox in July or August, you might like to go to a concert of classical music played by the orchestra.

Look for the instruments hidden in the tangled woods. Color all the ones you can find.

MASSACHUSETTS SCRAPBOOK

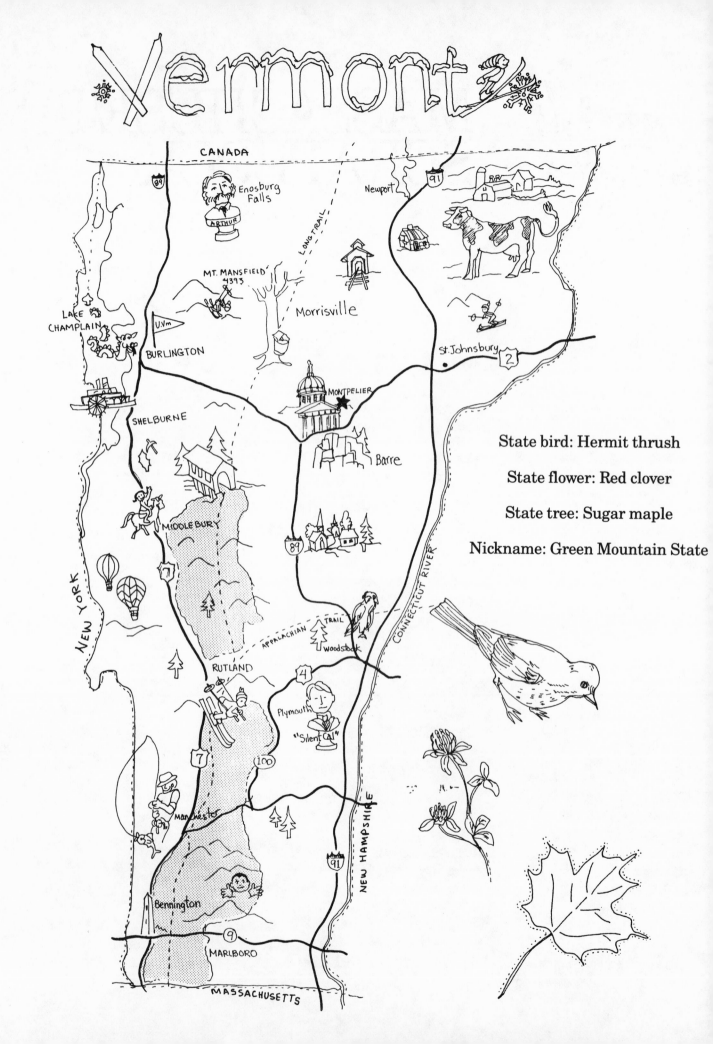

State bird: Hermit thrush

State flower: Red clover

State tree: Sugar maple

Nickname: Green Mountain State

What New England state has a French name?

Vermont means green ("vert," say: vayr) mountain ("mont") in French. It was a French explorer, Samuel de Champlain, who discovered this state in 1609. There are lots of towns with French names—like Calais (say: cal-LAY), Isle La Motte (say: EEL-la-MOT), Vergennes (say: ver-GENZ). Many Vermonters came from the French-speaking part of Canada. And at one ski area, Jay Peak, you will see as many license plates from Quebec as you do from New England.

Despite the French influence, Vermont is very much like the rest of New England. It was Vermonters, like President Calvin Coolidge, who made all Americans admire Yankee virtues, such as common sense and thrift.

This is the most rural state in America. In many ways, Vermont still looks the way the rest of New England did 50 years or even a century ago. You will see old-fashioned covered bridges (even a bridge that floats), lots of farms, and hand-painted signs everywhere (no billboards are allowed).

As one school girl said, "I like Vermont because the trees are close together, and the people are far apart." The biggest city, Burlington, is smaller than most of Boston's suburbs.

Vermont's State Animal

A new breed of horse got its start here, when Justin Morgan, a Vermont teacher, came home with a small yearling in payment for a debt owed him. "Figure" grew up to outrun and outperform bigger horses. You might enjoy reading Marguerite Henry's *Justin Morgan Had A Horse*. Or visit the University of Vermont's Morgan Horse Farm in Middlebury.

Figure was called a Morgan horse after his owner. Strong, dependable Morgans helped plow Vermont farms before there were tractors. As settlers began to move West, they rode Morgans or used this breed to pull their wagons. Today they are a favorite horse for policemen and park rangers to ride. They also make excellent family horses!

You will also see plenty of cows grazing on Vermont's gentle green mountains. It is fun to watch milk become cheese at Cabot's Creamery or sample homemade ice cream at Ben and Jerry's Factory.

Vermont's State Tree

Did you know Vermont is the largest manufacturer of maple products in the US? No wonder the sugar maple is the state tree. Spring is a fun time to visit here. You can still ski—and tour the state's sugar houses, as well! Be sure to try sugar-on-snow (real Vermont maple syrup hardened on soft, fresh snow).

Sap from maple trees is made into sugar candy and syrup. It takes a lot of sap to get the finished product, which is why you will see so many buckets attached to trees. Some sugar houses use miles of tubing to collect the sap from the trees. Look for sugar houses in Vermont—these are good places to learn how syrup is made (and you might get a taste, for free).

Vermont's Mountains

Vermont is a fun place to explore the outdoors. Its mountains are very old and much gentler than other peaks (like the Whites, next door in New Hampshire). It's fun to hike these mountains!

Vermont is shaped a little like a foot, with the heel down in Massachusetts and the toes up toward Canada. Can you draw a green line on the state map to show where there are trails for people to hike? (Hint: Hiking trails appear as dotted lines on most maps.) Where else do you see hiking trails in this book? Where have you hiked? You deserve a medal! Just color and cut out the hiking badge on page 91.

You may want to hike the Appalachian Trail or the Long Trail, which continues up the spine of Vermont's peaks to Canada. Or try other trails recommended by the Green Mountain Club ("Places to Go" in the back of this book will show you how to get good hiking and trail maps).

There are some important rules to remember whenever you go hiking. One is "be prepared." (Where have you heard that before?) In New England, this means to bring a canteen of water along, even on a short hike, and something to wear in case it rains. The weather changes very quickly here.

The second rule is "carry out what you bring in." In other words, don't litter. You want to keep these mountains green, don't you?

When the Green Mountains Turn White

You might also want to ski in Vermont. If you lived here, your school would take you to a local ski area to learn to snowplow or schuss down a hill. No wonder there are so many skiers in this state!

Like Maine and New Hampshire, Vermont has some of the best skiing in America. Stowe is an old-fashioned ski resort; the Trapp family, made famous in *The Sound of Music,* came here years ago to run an inn. Killington has the longest ski runs, while monadnocks (say: mo-NAD-nocks) like Burke Mountain and Ascutney are popular with families.

> Did you know monadnock means single, isolated mountain? These mountains, found in Vermont and New Hampshire, were formed later than the Green Mountains.

You can ski almost the whole length of this state—just the way you can hike it. The Catamount Trail Association is blazing a cross-country track that will be a skier's Long Trail by the year 2000. Already there are groomed intermediate trails through the wilderness, but within a day's run of inns.

There are two kinds of skis to try. Cross-country (also known as Nordic) is a little like sliding standing up. You use long, skinny skis and can even ski easily up a hill. You can go anywhere there is snow on cross-country skis.

Downhill or Alpine skis are softer, shorter, and easier to turn, so you can carve perfect "S" turns down a steep hill. Most people only use downhill skis where they can get a ride up the mountain on a lift. Which kind do you like best? T-bar, chairlift or gondola? Most Alpine ski areas can make snow, if the weather doesn't provide it.

Skiing is just one sport that Vermonters enjoy during the long, cold winter. You will see as many snowmobile crossing signs here as there are cow crossings. Hardy New Englanders also like to backpack in the winter, fish on frozen lakes, or snowshoe.

> Did you know that one year Vermont never got a summer? In 1816, a foot of snow fell in June, and it snowed in July and August. No wonder Vermonters have learned to make the most of cold weather!

A Lake That Was Once A Sea

It wasn't always cold here. Scientists have found fossils of coral, tiny animals that live in warm sea water, here in Vermont. And a whale fossil was discovered near Lake Champlain.

If you look at the map of New England, you will see that Vermont is the only state not on the Atlantic Ocean. But it was next to an ocean once long ago. Over millions of years, land shifted and moved. The Green Mountains pushed up (much the way a rug rises in the middle if you push the ends together). Vermont's ocean became a long, very deep lake.

Even today, the lake is so deep that it doesn't freeze until late winter. Lake Champlain would be a good place for a lake serpent to hide. But if Vermont has a monster living in Lake Champlain, it must be a friendly one, don't you think?

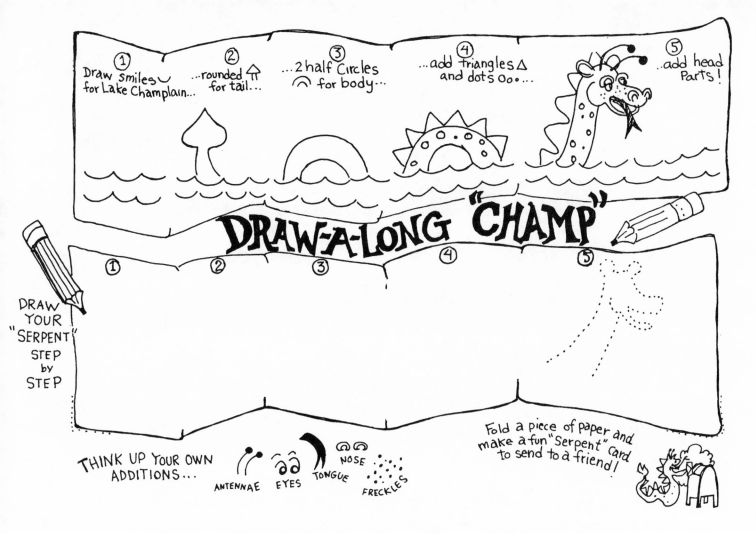

Lake Champlain is very deep. It would be a good place for a friendly monster to live. Since "Champ" is not real, you can use your imagination to create your own serpent.

SPRING

The Four Seasons in FALL

SUMMER

New England to Color

WINTER

TREE SEARCH

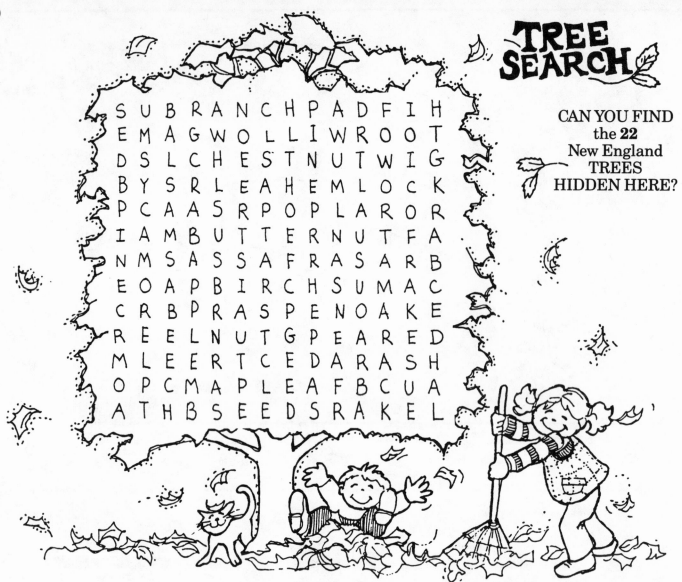

CAN YOU FIND the **22** New England TREES HIDDEN HERE?

```
S U B R A N C H P A D F I H
E M A G W O L L I W R O O T
D S L C H E S T N U T W I G
B Y S R L E A H E M L O C K
P C A A S R P O P L A R O R
I A M B U T T E R N U T F A
N M S A S S A F R A S A R B
E O A P B I R C H S U M A C
C R B P R A S P E N O A K E
R E E L N U T G P E A R E D
M L E E R T C E D A R A S H
O P C M A P L E A F B C U A
A T H B S E E D S R A K E L
```

New England Trees

ASH	MAPLE
ASPEN	OAK
BALSAM	PEAR
BEECH	PINE
BIRCH	POPLAR
BUTTERNUT	SASSAFRAS
CEDAR	SPRUCE
CHESTNUT	SUMAC
CRABAPPLE	SYCAMORE
ELM	TAMARACK
HEMLOCK	WILLOW

(Hint: 2 words are backwards, 1 word is diagonal, 2 are upside down, 1 word is in two places)

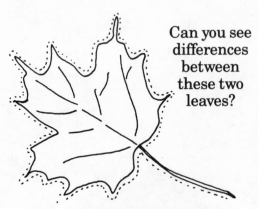

Can you see differences between these two leaves?

The **Sugar Maple** is Vermont's state tree. It is from the sap of this tree that maple sugar and maple syrup are made!

Rhode Island's state tree, the **Red Maple,** is also known as the Swamp Maple!

Bonus Words

BARK	NUT	SEEDS
BRANCH	ROOT	TREE
LEAF	SAP	TWIG
		RAKE

MAPLE SUGARING

In spring when the days are warm and sunny but the nights remain cold, it is sugaring season. This is the time of year when Vermonters load up trucks and sleds with spouts and buckets.

The Brown family has 20 sugar maples to tap. 10 trees are large enough to hold 2 buckets each. 5 maples are even bigger, and each take 3 buckets. 5 smaller, younger trees can only take 1 bucket. How many buckets did the Browns use?

A bucket full of sap weighs about 30 pounds. Could you carry a bucket that heavy without spilling it?

How many buckets can you count on this page?

The Browns are lucky. They have a sugar shack on their farm. They plan to turn sap into maple syrup. Neighbors bring sap from their trees to add to what the Browns have gathered. In all, there are 700 gallons of sap to boil into syrup. That is a lot of sap!

Does it make a lot of syrup? It takes 35 gallons of sap to make just one gallon of syrup. How many gallons of syrup did the Browns make at their sugar shack?

Morgan Horse

Vermont music teacher Justin Morgan got a sturdy little horse in payment for a debt. "Figure" sired the first American breed of horse. Known for their strength, Morgans pulled plows and carried Pony Express riders. Because they are also quick and smart, they make good police, polo, and show horses.

Color "Figure" and Justin Morgan.

VERMONT SCRAPBOOK

64

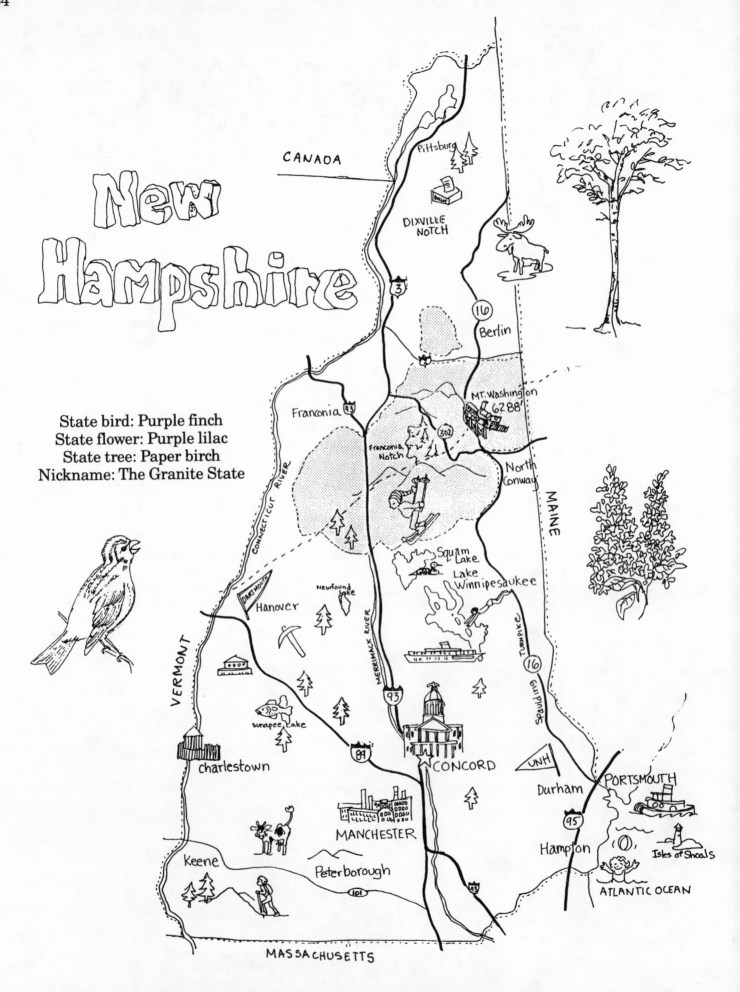

New Hampshire

CANADA

Pittsburg

DIXVILLE NOTCH

Berlin

State bird: Purple finch
State flower: Purple lilac
State tree: Paper birch
Nickname: The Granite State

Franconia

93

Mt. Washington 6288'

302

Franconia Notch

North Conway

MAINE

CONNECTICUT RIVER

Squam Lake

Lake Winnipesaukee

DARTMOUTH

Hanover

Newfound Lake

MERRIMACK RIVER

Spaulding Turnpike

16

VERMONT

Sunapee Lake

89

93

Charlestown

CONCORD

UNH

PORTSMOUTH

Durham

95

MANCHESTER

Hampton

Isles of Shoals

Keene

Peterborough

101

93

ATLANTIC OCEAN

MASSACHUSETTS

If you enjoy the outdoors, the Granite State is the place to be. In winter, you can ski, skate, snowshoe, even camp out at an Appalachian Mountain Club shelter. In warmer weather, there are trails everywhere: through cool pine woods, along crystal lakes, and up some of the highest peaks in New England.

Just be prepared for changes in the weather. It's been known to snow on the top of Mount Washington in July! This mountain is the highest point in the Northeast—and one of the few places in the US where Alpine plants grow.

Would you rather be at the ocean? Well, New Hampshire may have the shortest coastline of any state on the Atlantic Ocean, but it has some of the best beaches!

Look for a "drowned forest" near Odiorne Point State Park in Rye. To find out how trees could drown, continue reading.

The Glaciers at Work

The work of the great ice sheets or glaciers (say: GLAY-sherz) thousands and thousands of years ago can best be seen in the Granite State. Scientists think that New Hampshire was covered with ice and snow at least four different times. Some of these ice sheets were a mile thick!

When the climate got warmer, the ice melted and the earth pushed up—much like the way a sponge expands when it's wet. The water from the melting ice filled the holes in the earth left by the glaciers—that's why there are so many lakes in New Hampshire. Low-lying areas along the coast were also flooded. No wonder some trees drowned.

When the glaciers returned with colder weather, there were other changes. Moving ice sheets carried chunks of rock from the mountains southward. When the ice finally melted for good, the rocks were left scattered about the countryside.

Boulders and rocks moved by the glaciers are called erratics.

You will see many, many boulders in New Hampshire. The biggest one is outside Conway. It weighs 8,000 tons and is more than 80 feet long. How heavy is 8,000 tons? About as heavy as 20,000 pianos.

Strawberries Ahoy!

Did you know that explorers and fishermen discovered New Hampshire before the Pilgrims landed in Plymouth? The first settlers lived near the rivers and ocean because in those days it was easier to travel by water than by land.

When colonists came to Portsmouth, they called it Strawbery Banke because there were so many wild berries growing next to the river. It became a rich port and the capital of the colony.

Do you notice anything funny about the early name for Portsmouth? The colonists knew how to spell, but the English language has changed over the years. You may see strange-looking letters in old burying grounds here, or in old books. The colonial "s" looks a lot like our "f".

Portsmouth is on the Piscataqua River (say: Pis-CAT-uh-kwuh)—a river so salty and with such a strong current that it rarely freezes, no matter how cold the winters might get. This means that boats can use the port all year long.

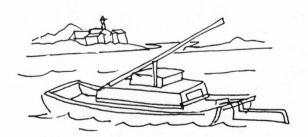

Big boats can't go very far up the river because it is shallow. In colonial times flat-bottomed boats, called gundalows, carried goods from ships anchored at sea up the river to inland towns.

Crystals in the Hills

The first American settler to explore the White Mountains was Darby Field, from Exeter. When he returned from his journey he showed people shiny rocks he had discovered in the mountains. Field thought they were rare crystals, but they really were just pieces of quartz—nice to look at, but not very valuable.

When you hike through the "Crystal Hills," as the colonists called the White Mountains, look for shiny rocks—they will probably be quartz. There are plenty of good places to look for crystals here. At Ruggles Mine, outside Andover, you can even rent rock picks and "collect" some mineral samples yourself!

The White Mountains

After the Revolutionary War, pioneers began to settle in the White Mountains. It was hard work clearing the land and building roads through the notches, but the people who moved to the mountains were as tough and rugged as the mountains themselves.

You can drive or hike over one early road that connects the town of Sandwich with the road to Waterville Valley. Listen to the leaves of the balm trees that the settlers planted for their music. (Hint: They look like poplar trees.) And see if you can find Cow Cave near a waterfall. One winter a farmer's cow kept warm under the rock ledge here.

Long ago two men trying to build a road through Franconia Notch came upon an enormous cliff on the side of a mountain. It resembles a face if you look at it sideways. This profile is known as the Old Man of the Mountain.

Count how many times you can find the Old Man of the Mountain in New Hampshire. (Hint: Look along the roadside.)

You will also see a lot of stone walls in this state, because when the settlers cleared the land to grow crops, they dug up lots of rocks and boulders left by the glaciers. They piled the rocks at the edges of their fields and later built fences with them to keep their animals from straying. How many stone walls did you see today?

When loggers began to cut trees in New Hampshire, sometimes they cut down too many. They were ruining the land and polluting the rivers with sawdust from their mills. That's why there are now laws to protect forests. Can you imagine the White Mountains with no trees?

Granite Staters are also working hard to preserve wildlife. The golden trout almost died off completely because of pollution, but thanks to people who cared, these fish can now be found in many of New Hampshire's lakes. People have made it easier for Atlantic salmon to swim up New Hampshire's rivers to lay their eggs—they built fish ladders next to dams. And because there are so many fish in the lakes, you might find our nation's bird, the bald eagle, looking for lunch in one of them.

ANIMAL TRACKS IN THE WOODS

HSSWOOEN BRIBTA

ERED

OCRNOAC

KKNSU

BOBCAT

SNOWSHOE RABBIT

MOUSE

SKUNK

DEER

BIRD

RACCOON

Actual tracks are rarely perfect. The best time to look for them is after it rains or snows!

PORCUPINE

EIPOPCNRU

ANIMAL SCRAMBLE

Unscramble the names of these forest friends. Find their tracks in the picture above.

OTBABC

XFODRE

SEMUO

MT. WASHINGTON, MAZE!

Mount Washington is the highest mountain in New England. Life at the top is a little different than at the bottom.

For instance, it could be snowing up there in July when it's steamy hot in the valley below.

In winter, you can expect 15 feet of snow to fall, and it is often the coldest place in the United States.

The strongest winds in the world were recorded on the summit of Mount Washington—231 miles per hour!

Would you like to take a train to the top? You can take the Cog Railway (watch out for the cinders from the smokestack). Pretend you're the engineer. Do you think you can find your way from the bottom to the top in this maze?

Or you could take the Auto Road (make sure your car has good brakes). Pretend you're the driver. Can you find your way to the top through the maze?

There are lots of trails that go up Mount Washington, but don't even think of climbing this mountain without experienced hikers to lead the way!

Old Stoneface

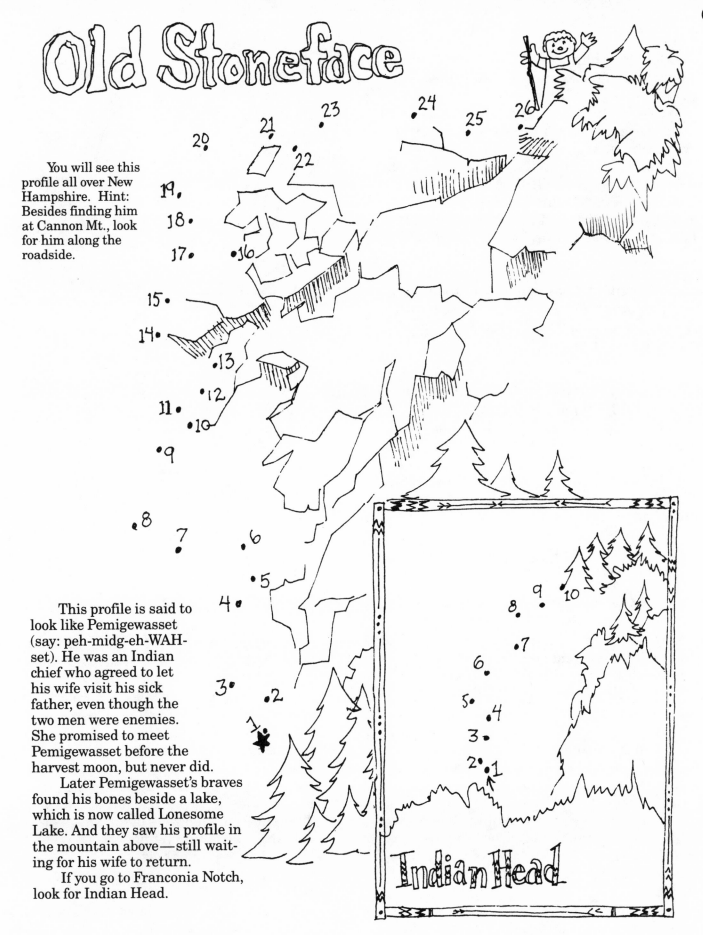

You will see this profile all over New Hampshire. Hint: Besides finding him at Cannon Mt., look for him along the roadside.

This profile is said to look like Pemigewasset (say: peh-midg-eh-WAH-set). He was an Indian chief who agreed to let his wife visit his sick father, even though the two men were enemies. She promised to meet Pemigewasset before the harvest moon, but never did.

Later Pemigewasset's braves found his bones beside a lake, which is now called Lonesome Lake. And they saw his profile in the mountain above—still waiting for his wife to return.

If you go to Franconia Notch, look for Indian Head.

Indian Head

Connect the dots and draw two faces you can see in the mountains of New Hampshire.

You don't have to go to the ocean to enjoy a beach. Visit a lake in New Hampshire, instead.

New Hampshire has wonderful lakes and ponds with all sorts of things to do. If you go swimming in a lake, you may find the water is not as cold as it is in the ocean. How else is a lake different from an ocean?

Besides swimming, you may want to canoe, fish, or water ski at a New England lake. And you can always sit still, look, and listen. What do you think you might discover at a lake or pond?

Who Am I? (Look carefully at the lake on the next page. Match the stories below with the plants and animals you see in the picture on the opposite page.)

I am an excellent engineer. I cut trees and limbs with my sharp teeth. Then I build a home for my family with trees and mud. After I'm finished building, I keep busy storing food for winter. I am a _ _ a _ _ _ .

I like the deep mud of lake shallows and pond bottoms. I am often the first sign of life after the ice melts every spring. But I am most important as a home—an apartment house, really—for dragonflies, moths, and other insects. I am an _ _ r _ _ h _ _ _ _ .

I love damp places—under logs or wet leaves. I lay my eggs in ponds and lakes. When I first crawl out in March or April, I am a sure sign that spring is here! Though I am very small, there are so many of my kind that together we outweigh all the birds and mammals that live near New Hampshire's lakes. What am I? A _ a l _ m _ _ d _ _ , of course.

Sensing the vibrations in the water helps me catch my food. And to get away in time, when someone is trying to catch me! I am a lake _ _ _ _ _ who doesn't want to get hooked.

I float through life—completely rootless. This habit allows me to go where others cannot. I like the cool, dark water of a deep lake rather than the warmer water of a shallow pond. I am a _ _ _ _ g b _ _ _ plant.

I'm not very quick, but I don't need to be. I carry my protection around wherever I go. Sometimes I lay my eggs in deserted muskrat lodges, where no one can find them. I am a painted t _ _ r _ _ _ _ .

Much like my saltwater cousins, I anchor myself with my foot to the muddy floor of a pond or lake. I eat tiny bits of food from water I take into my body. If the water becomes polluted, it gets hard for me to breathe. I am a freshwater _ _ _ _ .

I am one of the world's oldest living creatures. My kind have been around for at least 300 million years! I am born in water and live there until I am ready to fly. In the water, I eat insects, tadpoles, and tiny fish. Fully grown, I devour thousands of mosquitoes. I am a _ r _ _ _ n _ _ _ _ .

I hunt under water, even though I need air to breath. Like a well-equipped diver, I carry my own supply of air along with me. Only I use air bubbles instead of air tanks! I am a water _ p _ _ e _ .

New Hampshire's lakes are welcoming me once more. At Squam, people are so "crazy" about me that they have made some islands and inlets off limits to boaters and swimmers—because I need my privacy! I guess they love the sound of my voice—hooting, wailing, or yodeling. They say *my* voice is different from all others of my kind—as individual as each human fingerprint! What am I? A _ _ _ _ , what else?

I have webbed feet and powerful legs for swimming. My flat tail makes a rudder to help me turn quickly underwater. I catch lots of fish. Trout is my favorite! I hope you have as much fun in New Hampshire as I do! I'm an _ _ _ _ _ r .

Take a Closer LOOK at a N.H. Lake

Otter

Bullfrog

Loon

Beaver

Dragonfly

Frogbit plant

Painted turtle

Water Spider

Arrowhead

Salamander

Lake trout

Freshwater clam

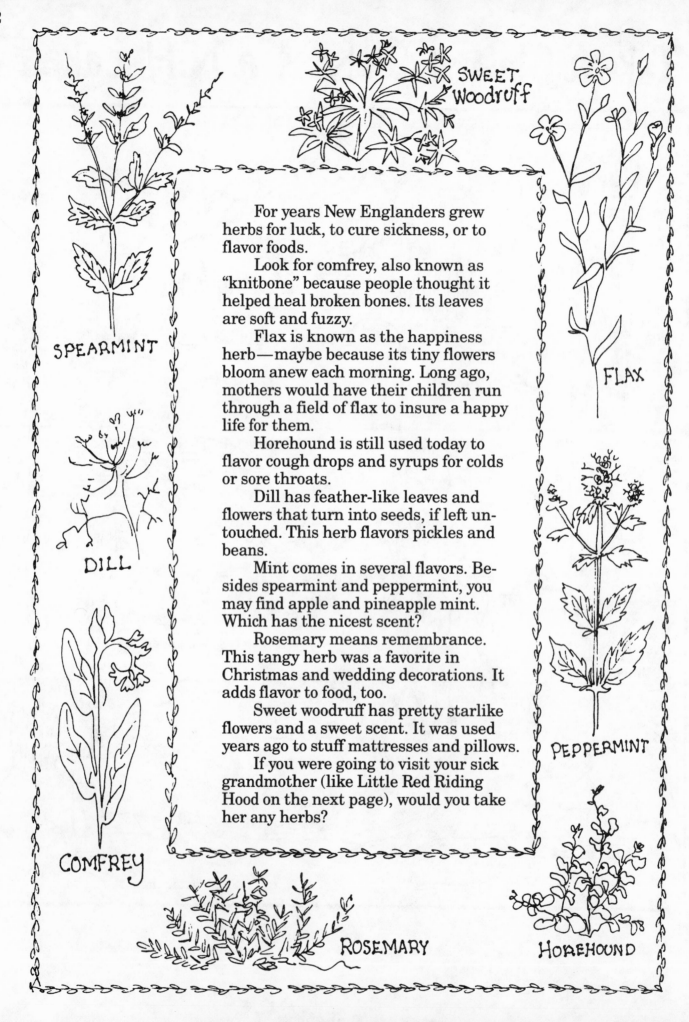

SWEET Woodruff

SPEARMINT

FLAX

DILL

PEPPERMINT

COMFREY

ROSEMARY

HOREHOUND

For years New Englanders grew herbs for luck, to cure sickness, or to flavor foods.

Look for comfrey, also known as "knitbone" because people thought it helped heal broken bones. Its leaves are soft and fuzzy.

Flax is known as the happiness herb—maybe because its tiny flowers bloom anew each morning. Long ago, mothers would have their children run through a field of flax to insure a happy life for them.

Horehound is still used today to flavor cough drops and syrups for colds or sore throats.

Dill has feather-like leaves and flowers that turn into seeds, if left untouched. This herb flavors pickles and beans.

Mint comes in several flavors. Besides spearmint and peppermint, you may find apple and pineapple mint. Which has the nicest scent?

Rosemary means remembrance. This tangy herb was a favorite in Christmas and wedding decorations. It adds flavor to food, too.

Sweet woodruff has pretty starlike flowers and a sweet scent. It was used years ago to stuff mattresses and pillows.

If you were going to visit your sick grandmother (like Little Red Riding Hood on the next page), would you take her any herbs?

Pickity Place

The farmhouse at Pickity Place is where the drawings for one popular version of LITTLE RED RIDING HOOD were made. You will see a wolf in grandmother's bed in one room here.

Can you help Little Red Riding Hood safely find her way to her real grandmother? Watch out for that clever wolf!

74

Find the P's in Portsmouth!

NEW HAMPSHIRE SCRAPBOOK

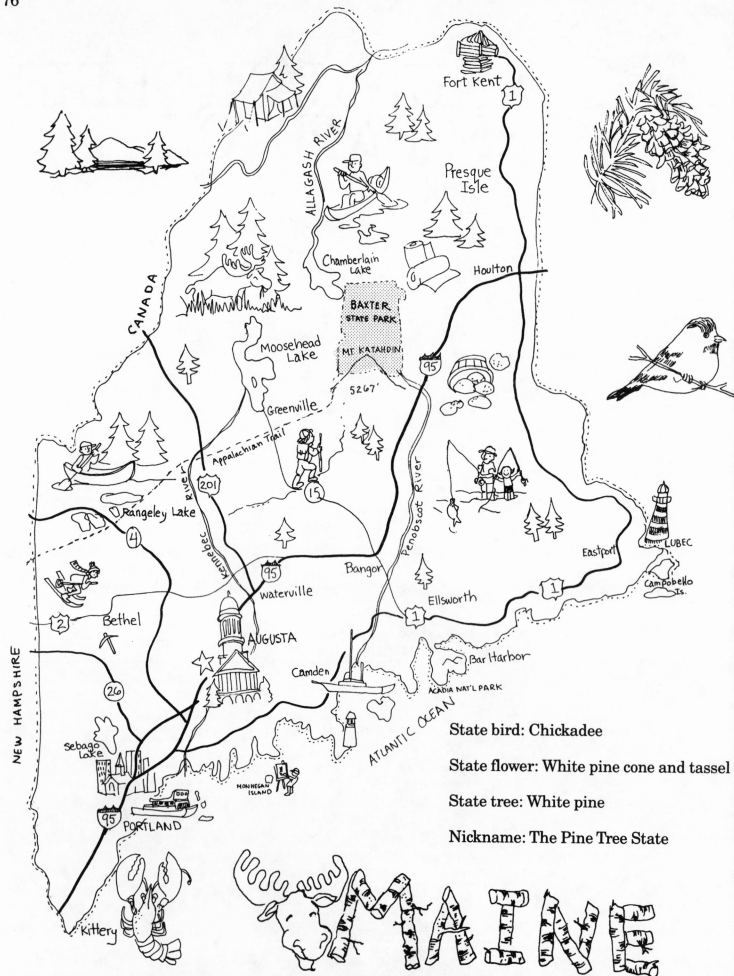

Fort Kent

Presque Isle

ALLAGASH RIVER

CANADA

Chamberlain Lake

Houlton

BAXTER STATE PARK

MT. KATAHDIN

Moosehead Lake

5267'

Greenville

Appalachian Trail

95

201

Kennebec River

Penobscot River

Rangeley Lake

4

Eastport

LUBEC

Campobello Is.

15

Bethel

2

95

Waterville

Bangor

Ellsworth

1

NEW HAMPSHIRE

26

AUGUSTA

Camden

Bar Harbor

ACADIA NAT'L PARK

ATLANTIC OCEAN

Sebago Lake

MONHEGAN ISLAND

95

PORTLAND

Kittery

State bird: Chickadee

State flower: White pine cone and tassel

State tree: White pine

Nickname: The Pine Tree State

MAINE

Maine's Skyscrapers

There are so many pine trees in Maine, they decided to call it the "Pine Tree State."

Maine is almost as big as all the other New England states put together. Almost all of it is filled with pine trees. There are enough pine trees here to cover 17 million football fields. Not many people live in the huge pine forests—just a few lumber workers and their families.

People who like being alone come to these woods to hunt, fish, and camp—or just to enjoy looking at the tall trees. One visitor said the pine trees were so tall that "the clouds were torn as they passed over them."

You might think the roads through the forests would be empty, but you will pass many trucks full of pine logs. These trucks carry logs to mills, where they are cut up into timber or ground into pulp for newspapers and paper napkins. Look around to see how many things could have come from a pine tree.

Maine = H$_2$0

If anything is more important to Maine than pine trees, it is water.

Imagine Maine without it. There would be no waves crashing against the rocks. No puffins. No lighthouses. No seals. No ferries. No lakes or ponds. No rivers or streams. No sailboats or canoes. No tides. No lobsters. What would there be? Pine trees!

Lucky for us, Maine still has plenty of water and everything that goes with it. West Quoddy Head has the highest tides in the country. Here, you can be the first person in the US to see the sun rise, because Quoddy Head is as far east as you can go in this country.

If you visit West Lubec or Pembroke, you can see waterfalls that go in one direction when the tide comes in, and the opposite direction when it goes out.

Thousands of years ago, New England was covered with thick ice sheets. When they melted, much of Maine's coastline was flooded. About 2,000 mountains ended up as islands. Many mountain ridges were left with water on three sides, forming peninsulas. They look like fingers of land reaching into the sea. (If you want to know more about peninsulas and islands, turn to page 87.)

In parts of Maine, it's easier to travel from one place to another by boat than by car. For example, to get from the town of Eastport to Lubec is only three miles by sea—but it's 40 miles by car!

Which is longer in distance, following the coast of Maine from one end to the other, or traveling across the country? The coast of Maine has so many peninsulas that it is actually farther to drive along its coast than to cross the country!

Along the Maine coast there are 60 lighthouses warning sailors to steer clear of cliffs and islands in their path. Chances are, you won't be far from one in your travels through the state. (There's a lighthouse you can color on page 84.)

Do you like fresh water? There's plenty of that in Maine, too. This state has 6,000 lakes and ponds for fishing, and almost as many rivers and streams. The biggest lakes are Moosehead and Sebago. But even the small ones have enough room for fishermen, waterskiers, loons, and a moose or two.

Lake water in Maine is warmer and softer than sea water. Still, you can't expect it to be like hopping into your bathtub. These lakes take some getting used to. Stick your toes in first.

If Maine's lakes are too cold to swim in, you can still enjoy just looking at them from a distance. One of the best places to look is from the top of Mt. Katahdin, Maine's highest peak. You can see hundreds of lakes and ponds in all directions, with no other mountains to block your view. Henry David Thoreau, who spent a lot of time outdoors, compared the view of Maine's lakes among the pine trees to a "huge mirror that had shattered, with glittering bits thrown on the grass."

78

Furry, Feathered, and Human Mainers

People from all over the US and many foreign countries come to Maine. Some stay—others are just visiting, but wish they could stay.

There are many towns in Maine named after foreign cities or countries. (One of the names on this list is a real town in Maine, but doesn't belong here. Can you find it?) Norway, Paris, Denmark, Naples, Sweden, Poland, Mexico, Meddybemps, Peru, China, Athens, Belgrade, Bremen, Carthage, Corinth, Dresden, Frankfort, Hanover, Lebanon, Lisbon, Madrid, Moscow, Palermo, Rome, Sorrento, Stockholm, Troy, Verona, Vienna.

One of Maine's most famous visitors was a furry creature who would swim every year from Boston to his summer home in Rockland. His name was Andre the Seal. In the winter, when the ocean is icy cold, he enjoyed the warmth of the New England Aquarium. But in summer, he would bask in the sunshine on the coast of Maine—just as many human visitors do. If you go to Rockland, you will see a granite statue of Andre, facing the island where he was born.

Some year-round residents in Maine are birds and animals not found in other parts of the country. Do you know what blue jays look like? In the back woods, you may see Canada jays. They don't look at all like blue jays, but they act just as feisty. They are so bold, they will take food right off a picnic table—even with hungry people around. Anyone lost in the woods would like these jays because they often lead people back to civilization. Of course, the birds are just looking for bacon and eggs to eat up.

If you take the ferry to Matinicus Rock or Machias Seal Island, there's another year-round resident of Maine you can see—a puffin. It's a bird that nests on high cliffs overlooking the ocean. He's also called a "sea parrot" because of his brightly-colored, triangle-shaped bill.

Someone who liked Maine's animals very much was Rachel Carson. She wrote a book called *Silent Spring*. It told how pollution from insecticides was killing our wildlife. Her work made us see how important all creatures are. All life works together to keep New England and our world the wonderful place it is. We must understand that animals and plants have as much right to live as we humans do. We need to be careful not to hurt animals and plants. Do you think we're being careful enough?

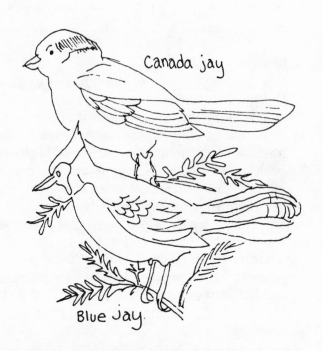

Canada jay

Blue Jay

MAINE'S WILDLIFE

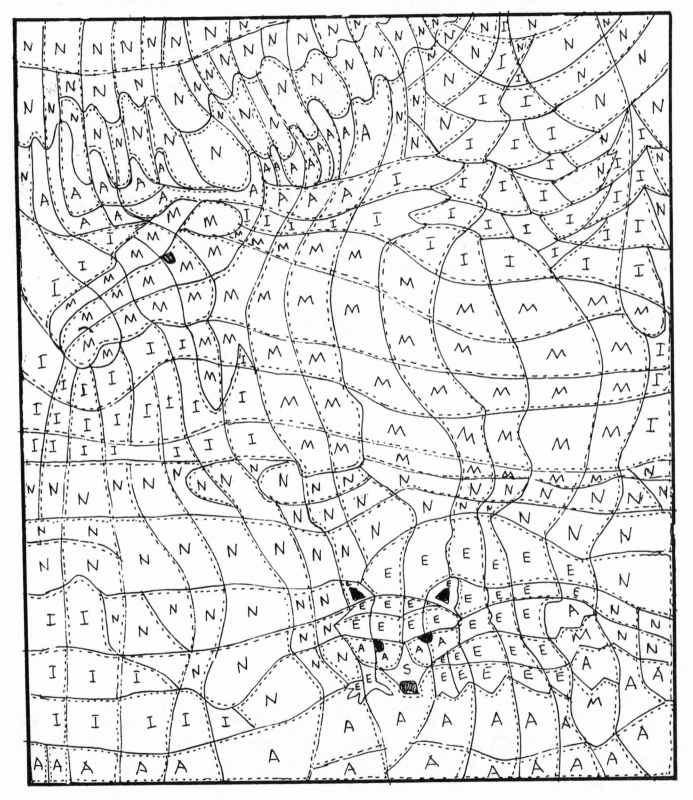

Color this page using this code.

M = BROWN A = BLACK I = GREEN N = BLUE E = GREY

Design a New England House.

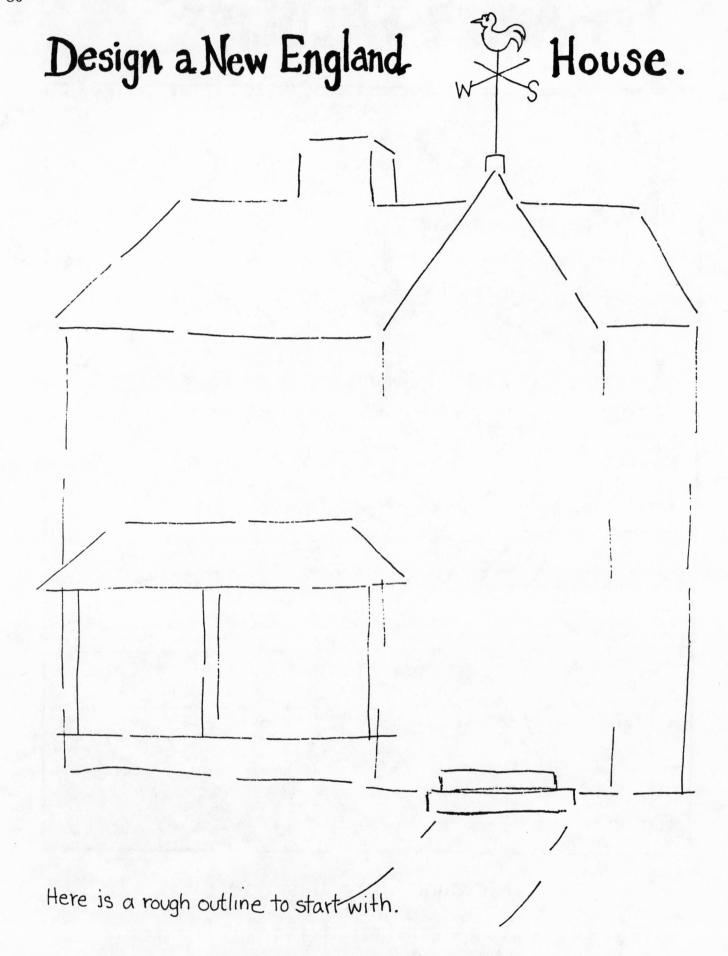

Here is a rough outline to start with.

Wedding Cake House

This old home is known as the "Wedding Cake House" because its woodwork looks like icing on a cake. It is said that the ship captain who built this house in the 1800s wanted to make up to his wife for having to leave his own wedding before he cut their cake! (In the old days of sailing ships "time and tide" wouldn't wait for a honeymoon.)

Help the bride find her wedding gifts hidden in her "Cake House"!

Flowers
Mirror
Comb
Silverware
Hat
Money
Ring
Pearls
Parasol
Dishes
Goblets
Earrings

If you go east to Kennebunkport, pass through town, and drive along Ocean Avenue, you will finally come to another famous house. The large summer cottage on the ocean at Walker's Point belongs to President George Bush!

Salt Marsh

Cormorant

Red-Breasted merganser

Loggerhead turtle

Sea lettuce

Salt Hay

Sand shrimp

Reed

Black-backed gull

Sand spurry

Spike grass

Great blue heron

Red sponge

Goldeneye

Red crab

Green crab

Northern quahog

Rockweed

dog welk

Dulse

Muskrat

Steamer clam

Scarborough Marsh is Maine's largest salt marsh. You can rent
a canoe or hike along with a naturalist, who will help you find some
of the interesting plants and animals that live here.
Circle whatever you think lives in a New England salt marsh.

83

Sandpiper

Bladder wrack

Deer mouse

Sea walnut

Rock barnacle

Bald eagle

Sun jellyfish

Moon jellyfish

Irish moss

Periwinkle

Tufted sponge

Silverweed

Green sea urchin

Hermit crab

Kelp

Bay scallop

Shoveler

Blue mussel

Oyster

When you are visiting New England, you might try some of these:
Quahogs, steamers, oysters, mussels, scallops.
Did you know some people eat seaweed?

BUOYS + LIGHTHOUSES

People with sailboats love to visit Maine in the summer because the weather is cool and there is usually enough wind to push their boats. Also, there are many bays and inlets, where sailors can find protection from storms.

NUN

BELL

CAN

People who sail in strange waters need signals to warn them of shallow places or rocks hidden beneath the surface. These signals are called buoys. They come in all shapes and sizes—some even have bells that ring as they tip in the waves. Others have whistles. Still others have flashing lights. Sounds and lights make sailing safer in fog or at night.

Lighthouses keep sailors out of danger by flashing a bright light to warn of islands or cliffs. People used to live in lighthouses. They would turn on the light at night or when it was foggy. Nowadays, most lights can be turned on by radio signals from shore, so there is no need for lighthouse keepers anymore.

How would you like to live in a lighthouse? Wouldn't you like to take a boat to school? Would it be called a schoolboat? What color would it be?

PORTLAND HEAD LIGHT

If you and a friend learn Morse Code, you can send messages to each other by flashlight, just as some sailors do. Different combinations of short and long flashes stand for different letters. Here is the code for each letter of the alphabet:

A .-	G --.	N -.	T -
B -...	H	O ---	U ..-
C -.-.	I ..	P .--.	V ...-
D -..	J .---	Q --.-	W .--
E .	K -.-	R .-.	X -..-
F ..-.	L .-..	S ...	Y -.--
	M --		Z --..

Can you decipher this message?

- .. -- . ..-. --- .-. .-.. ..- -. -.-. ....

Another way to send messages is by putting a note in a bottle and letting it float on the ocean currents. Someday it may be found.

Two boys came upon a "bottle letter" on a beach in Maine. It was from a sailor whose ship had sunk in the Mediterranean Sea four years earlier!

Maine is a good place to send a message by bottle because the currents are strong. Here's how to do it:

Send a Bottle Message

• Find a thick glass bottle with a narrow neck—like a catsup or soda bottle. • Wash it well and let it dry. • Find a cork that will fit tightly in the neck of the bottle. (Test it in the bathtub to see if it really keeps the water out.) • When you have a cork that fits, write your message. Be sure to write when you sent your message and from where you sent it. Don't forget to include your name and address, so whoever finds the bottle can answer your note.

How far do you think the bottle will float? Have you ever found a bottle with a message inside? There could be thousands floating around out there.

ACADIA NATIONAL PARK

Acadia National Park is made up of two islands and one peninsula in Maine. Do you know the difference between a peninsula and an island?

A peninsula is land that juts out into the water. It has water all around it—except on *one* side.

An island is surrounded by water—on *all* sides.

Color the islands that you see on the map yellow and the peninsula orange.

You can only reach Isle Au Haut (say: EEL-oh-HOAT) by boat. But you can drive to the Schoodic Peninsula or sail a boat there. Most people drive to Mount Desert Island. How can you drive to an island? Over a bridge, of course. Mount Desert is close to the coast, so there is a bridge or causeway here.

Where would you rather live? On an island or on a peninsula? Why?

An Island That Became a Desert

Mount Desert Island is a good place to see some of the changes nature makes. Once upon a time, there were mountains here. Then the glaciers came.

The mountains sank beneath the weight of all that ice and snow. When the glaciers melted, most of the mountains were under water.

The glaciers scraped all the soil and plants off the land. New soil had to be made all over again.

Rocks which froze, cracked, and crumbled into sand helped to make soil. Lichens (say: LIE-kins) were the first plants to grow on Mount Desert. They make an acid that helps crack rocks to make more sand. When lichens die, they mix with sand to form soil.

Years later as more soil formed, mosses and ferns began to grow. When they died, they added to the soil, too. Slowly, more plants, flowers, shrubs, and finally trees followed the first plants on Mount Desert.

Millions and millions of years later, there were all sorts of growing things here. This island did not look like a desert, then!

In 1947 a fire quickly destroyed a large forest on Mount Desert. Because the wind was so strong, the flames moved fast. Fire spread over 10 miles in two hours. (Most people walk about 3 miles in an hour.)

Thousands of acres of forest were gone. But not for long!

If you visit Mount Desert now, you will see a new forest. How many years did it take these trees, shrubs, and plants to replace the ones burned by fire?

Plants grow in a certain order. After the fire, the first plants that appeared were shrubs and broadleaf trees—aspen, birch, and maple. When they began to make shade, evergreen trees could grow—firs, pines, and spruces.

The pictures below show the plants that helped to make soil after the glaciers and the plants that grew after the fire.

Put numbers in the boxes to show the order plants grew on Mount Desert. What was the first kind of plant to appear after the glaciers? The second? Which grew here first: flowers and shrubs or evergreen trees?

If you come back to Mount Desert Island when you are grown-up, you may see many more changes.

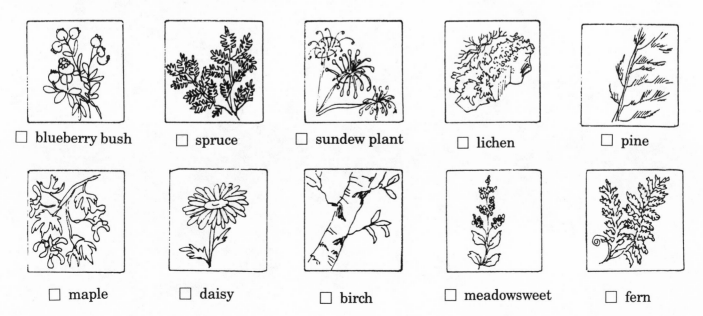

☐ blueberry bush   ☐ spruce   ☐ sundew plant   ☐ lichen   ☐ pine

☐ maple   ☐ daisy   ☐ birch   ☐ meadowsweet   ☐ fern

SUMMER CAMP

MAINE
SCRAPBOOK

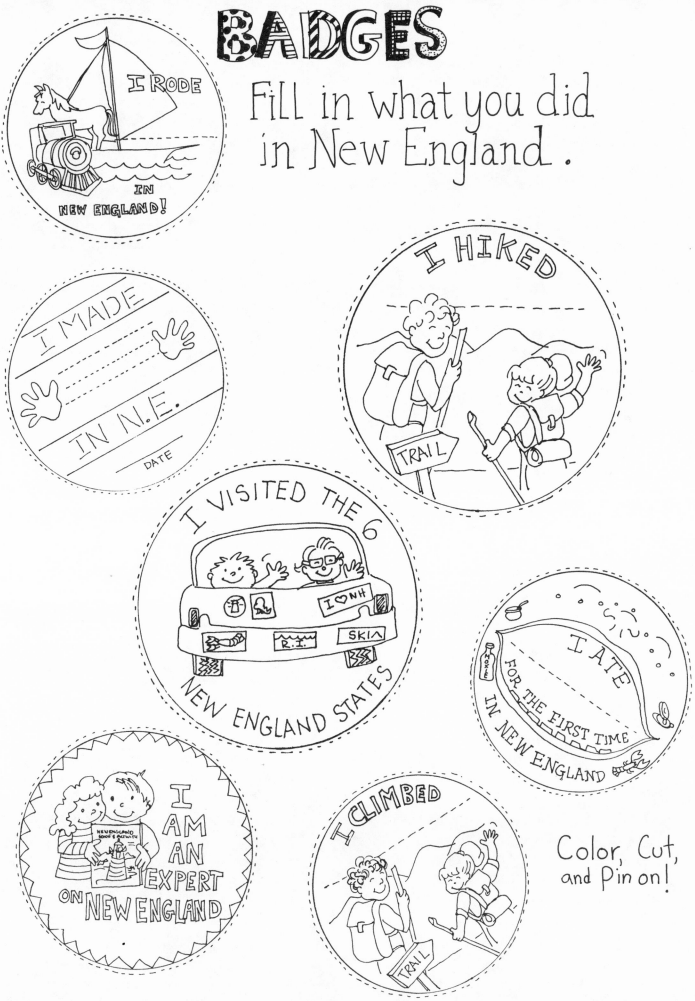

BADGES

Fill in what you did in New England.

I RODE IN NEW ENGLAND!

I MADE ___ IN N.E. ___ DATE

I HIKED

I VISITED THE 6 NEW ENGLAND STATES

I ♥ NH   R.I.   SKI

I ATE ___ FOR THE FIRST TIME IN NEW ENGLAND

I AM AN EXPERT ON NEW ENGLAND

I CLIMBED

TRAIL

Color, Cut, and Pin on!

ANSWERS

Page 8
Some words you can make from Connecticut:
cent coin cone cut cute connect continue
in it on one net no none not note tent tin
to toe ton tone tonic tot tote tune unite

From Constitution:
coin coot cots cotton count in no noon not
notion nut on onion so son soon sonic stout
suit tin tint ton toot tuition

Page 9

He was the largest ATHEPLEN ELEPHANT in the world!

Page 11

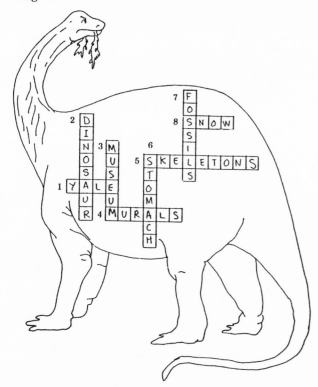

Page 13
One clock is missing one hand. Another clock has its
numbers going the wrong way.

Page 16

Page 18
A – Enlisted mess
B – Attack center
C – Officer's Wardroom
D – Bridge
E – Radio Room

Page 21.
The First Mate went from "B" to "C" and up
to the loft above, then to "S", and the *Morgan*. The
School Teacher went from "W" to "A", past the *Morgan*
and the *Emma C. Berry,* "R", and crossed the green
(near where the Children's Museum is today) before
returning to "W".

The First Mate started out with $16 ($10 in
currency, $6 in coin). If you subtract $3 for biscuits, $5
for canvas, and $4 for two cutting irons, there is only
$4 left—not enough for a new harpoon.

Did you spell cat, dinosaur, whale, Mystic, sloop,
and chair correctly?

Page 23
If you drive 60 miles per hour for one hour, you have
gone 60 miles.

Page 25

the Flying Horses of Watch Hill

Page 26

'X' Marks the Spot

Page 29
The code reads: What is your name? Write it below with flags.

Page 30

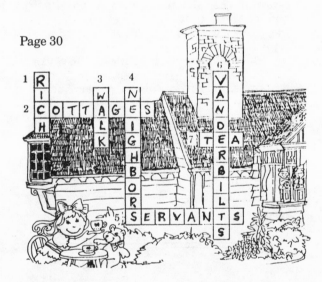

Page 32
Did you at find at least 35 wheels at Slater Mill?

Page 37
The sperm whale in this picture has 24 teeth.

Page 43

Ferries A, B, C, and D go between the mainland of Massachusetts and the islands of Martha's Vineyard and Nantucket. Can you figure out which ferry goes where? Look at the maze, and then put the correct letters in the spaces below:

1. Ferry C leaves Woods Hole and arrives at Nantucket Island.
2. Ferry B leaves New Bedford and arrives at Martha's Vineyard.
3. Ferry D leaves Hyannis and stops at Martha's Vineyard on the way to Nantucket Island.
4. Ferry A leaves New Bedford and arrives at Nantucket Island.

Pages 46 – 47

15 "Old Ironsides."
17 Watch out for the sharks.
8 "One if by land, two if by sea."
2 Home of the Red Sox.
3 Where Mr. & Mrs. Mallard & family live.

4 It has a gold dome.
21 You can see stars in the daytime here.
9 Home of the Bruins & Celtics.
1 This goes underground.
12 There's a grasshopper on top.

Pages 50 – 51
The air conditioner, balloons, baseball cap, bathing suit, Batman kite, car, chain-link fence, cooler, diet soda, digital clock, drive-in teller, frisbee, jet, lawnmower, light bulb, movies, parking meters, pizza, poodle, radio, shopping car, shorts or sneakers on a girl, skateboard, stop sign, swimming pool, tee-shirts, trailer, TV antenna, truck, and walkman would not have been found in Sturbridge 150 years ago.

Page 52

Page 60

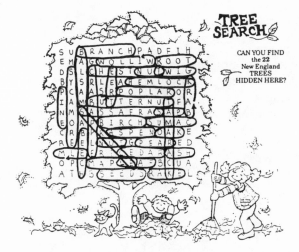

Page 61
The Browns have 40 buckets of syrup in all. There are 32 buckets in the picture, including those the Browns are carrying or holding. If it takes 35 gallons of sap to make one gallon of syrup, the Browns made 20 gallons of syrup from 700 gallons of sap.

Page 67

SNOWSHOE RABBIT

RACCOON

MOUSE

SKUNK

BOB CAT

DEER

RED FOX

PORCUPINE

Page 68

Page 69

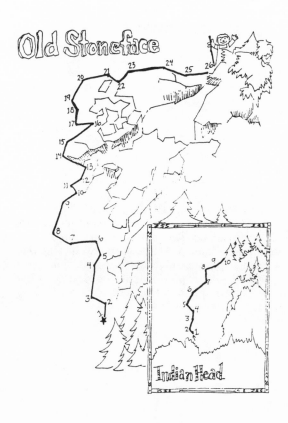

Page 70 – 71

"I am an excellent engineer. . . a *beaver.*"

"I like the deep mud of lake shallows. . . an *arrowhead.*"

"I love damp places—under logs or wet leaves. . . a *salamander.*"

"Sensing the vibrations in the water all about me and seeing to either side of me. . . lake *trout.*"

"I float through life—completely rootless. . . *frogbit* plant."

"Like my saltwater cousins, I anchor myself. . . a freshwater *clam.*"

"I am one of the world's oldest living creatures. . . a *dragonfly.*"

"I hunt under water, even though I need air to breathe. . . I am a water *spider.*"

"New Hampshire's lakes are welcoming me. . . A *loon,* what else?"

"I have webbed feet and powerful legs for swimming. . . an *otter.*"

Page 73

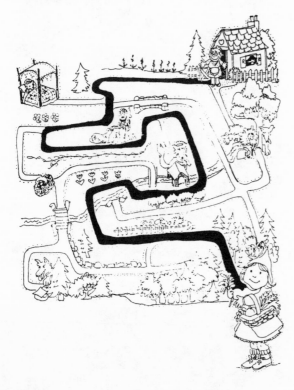

Page 74

Did you see these things that begin with "P" in Portsmouth? "P" on a tugboat, pail, painters, panda, pansies, parasol, peg leg, petunias, periscopes, photographer, piano, picket fence, picnic basket, pie, piers, pilings, pigeons, pigtails, pineapple, pinwheel, pipe, pirates, plants, playbill, pole, polka dots, pony tail, Pop's Lunch, pregnant woman, Prescott Park, print shop, pulleys, puppy.

Page 77

Meddybemps is the Maine town listed that is not also the name of a foreign city or country.

Page 78

Morse Code reads: TIME FOR LUNCH

Page 81

Page 84 – 85

All the plants and animals listed here can be found in a New England salt marsh.

Page 89

1: Lichen

2: Fern

3 – 5: Flowering plants (daisy, meadowsweet, sundew)

6: Bushes (blueberries) and shrubs

7 – 8: Hardwoods, like birch or maple trees

9 – 10: Evergreens, like pine or spruce

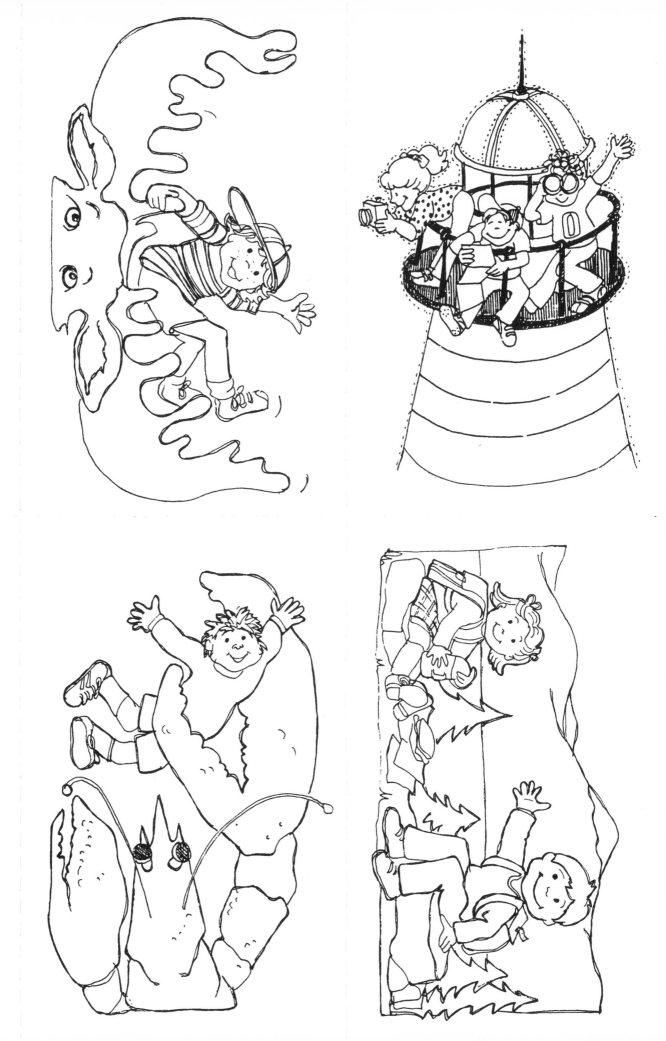

PLACE
POST CARD
POSTAGE
HERE

ZIP

PLACE
POST CARD
POSTAGE
HERE

ZIP

PLACE
POST CARD
POSTAGE
HERE

Zip

PLACE
POST CARD
POSTAGE
HERE

Zip

PLACES TO GO

GUIDE TO SYMBOLS

♪ Arts events (including plays or music)

&bike; Bike trails

⌣ Boating or canoeing

▲ Camping

✗ Cross-country skiing

⛷ Downhill skiing

🐟 Fishing

♿ Handicapped access

🥾 Hiking

? Information

❀ Nature area

🏕 Picnic area

🍴 Restaurant

🛍 Shop

🥤 Snack Bar

🏊 Swimming

Connecticut

Area code: 203
For information on state parks (unless otherwise noted), call 566-2304.

BLOOMFIELD

Airventures, 167 Duncaster Rd., offers FAA-certified hot-air balloon excursions year-round. Adm. 242-7327

Farm Implement Museum, 434 Tunxis Ave. (rte. 189N), exhibits early tools & offers hands-on activities; petting zoo. Free for preschoolers; open spring—fall. 242-7961

Penwood SP, rte. 185, 4 miles west of town, has 787 wooded acres to explore.

BRANFORD

Harrison House (c. 1720), 124 Main St. (Exits 53N/54S, I-95), is a restored saltbox. Free; open Wed.—Sat. in summer or by appt. 488-4828/-8835

"Puppet House" Theatre, 128 Thimble Island Rd. Closed in March. 481-3309

Sea Mist II (481-4841) & *Volsunga III* (488-9978 or 481-3345), Stony Creek Dock, offer narrated Thimble Island cruises; fare. Run spring—fall.

BRIDGEPORT

P.T. Barnum Museum, 820 Main St. (Exit 27, I-95), has recently been renovated. Adm.; closed Mon. 331-1104

Beardsley Zoological Gardens, Beardsley Park on Noble Ave. (Exit 27A, I-95), is state's largest zoo; pony rides. Parking fee; closed major holidays. 576-8082

Mr. Lucky cruises, Captain's Cove Seaport, 1 Bostwick Ave. (Exit 26, I-95), offers daily narrated excursions into the Sound. Fare. 335-1433

Museum of Art, Science & Industry, 4450 Park Ave. (Exit 27, I-95), has hands-on

activities for children. Adm.; closed Mon. 372-3521

HMS Rose, Captain's Cove Seaport, 1 Bostwick Ave. (Exit 26, I-95), is a replica of the British warship that caused colonists to found an American navy. Adm.; open spring—fall. 335-1433

BRISTOL

Am. Clock & Watch Museum, 100 Maple St. off rte. 6 (Exit 38W/31E, I-84), has over 1,800 timepieces; better for older kids. Adm. 8 yrs. & up; open spring—fall. 583-6070

H.C. Barnes Mem. Nature Center, 175 Shrub Rd., has displays plus live reptiles & amphibians. Free; closed Mon. 589-6082

Lake Compounce, rte. 229 (Exit 31, I-84), is a 40-acre theme park.

Plainville Hist. Center, 29 Pierce St. (Exit 34, I-84), Plainville, has clocks, costumes, toys, wagons. Donations; open spring—fall. 747-0705/-6577

BURLINGTON

Trout Hatchery, Belden Rd. off rte. 4, raises 90,000 pounds of trout each year. Free; open daily. 673-2340

CANAAN

Housatonic RR Co., Union Station (rtes. 7 & 44), is the oldest US train station in continuous use; sightseeing trips. Adm. 824-0339

CANTERBURY

Prudence Crandall House, Canterbury Green (rtes. 14 & 169), has changing exhibits in New England's first school for black girls (1833). Adm.; closed

mid-Dec. to mid-Jan. & Thanksgiving. 546-9916/-3005

CANTON

Canton Hist. Museum, 11 Front St. off rte. 179 in Collinsville, exhibits various 19th-century toys & tools; general store plus post office. Adm.; open spring—fall. 693-2793

Roaring Brook Nature Center, 70 Gracey Rd. off rte. 44, has Indian longhouse & live animals; 6 miles of self-guided trails. Open daily in summer (closed Mon. rest of year). 693-0263

CENTRAL VILLAGE

Quinebaug Valley Trout Hatchery, Cady Ln. (Exit 89, I-395), has a glass wall for viewing. Free; open daily.

CHESHIRE

Lock 12 Hist. Park, 487 N. Brooksvale (rte. 42), is restored section of Farmington Canal with museum & unusual bridge. Free; open daily, March—Nov. 272-2743

CORNWALL

Cornwall Bridge, rte. 128, W. Cornwall, is a covered bridge, rare in this part of NE.

Mohawk Mt. SP, rte. 4, 6 miles west of Goshen, offers year-round hiking in state's finest winter sports area.

COVENTRY

Nathan Hale Homestead, South St. off rte. 44, is a 1776 home with memorabilia of the famous patriot. Adm.; open spring—fall. 742-6917

DANBURY

Putnam Mem. SP, rtes. 58 & 107, Redding, has Rev. War museum. Free; museum open spring & summer, park year-round. 938-2285

Scott-Fanton Museum, 43 Main St. (Exit 5, I-84), has changing exhibits plus John Dodd (hat) Shop (c. 1790). Free; open Wed.—Sun. 743-5200

EAST GRANBY

McLean Game Refuge, rte. 10, Granby, offers recreation & nature study on a 3,400-acre sanctuary. Free; no pets.

Old New-Gate Prison & Copper Mine, Newgate Rd. (Exit 40, I-91), was a copper mine & prison. Free for preschoolers; open spring—fall. 653-3563/566-3005

EAST HADDAM

Devil's Hopyard SP, 3 miles north of rtes. 82 & 156, has 60' Chapman Falls plus potholes, said to be made by Devil hopping from ledge to ledge.

Nathan Hale Schoolhouse, Main St. (rte. 149) behind St. Stephen's Church, is the one-room school where Hale taught. Adm.; open in summer. 873-9547

EAST HAVEN

Shoreline Trolley Museum, 17 River St. (Exit 51N/52S, I-95), has 100 classic trolleys plus 3-mile shoreline ride. Adm.; open daily in summer. 467-6927

ESSEX

CT River Museum, at foot of Main St. (Exit 3, rte. 9), is an 1878 dockhouse with replica of America's first submarine, the *Turtle*. Adm.; open April—Dec. 767-8269

Museum of Fife & Drum, N. Main St. at Highland (Exit 3, rte. 9), may be just the place

for a child taking band; music, old instruments, uniforms. Kids free; open Fri.—Sun. spring—fall. 399-6519

Pratt House (1732-34), 19 West Ave. (Exit 3, Rte. 9), is a center-chimney colonial with period herb garden. Kids under 12 free; open Fri.—Sun. in summer. 767-0861

Valley RR, Railroad Ave. (Exit 3, rte. 9), is a vintage steam train that connects to Deep River steamboat cruise. Adm. 767-0103

FAIRFIELD

Birdcraft Museum & Sanctuary, 314 Unquowa Rd. (Exit 21, I-95), has kids' activity corner, dinosaur footprints, changing wildlife exhibits on small preserve. Adm.; open Thurs., Sat., Sun. year-round. 259-0416

CT Audubon Soc. Center, 2325 Burr St. (Exit 21, I-95), has 6 miles of trails on 160-acre sanctuary; singing & fragrance walk for blind & handicapped. Adm. for sanctuary, open daily; center free; closed Sun., Mon. & major holidays. 259-6305

Ogden House, 1520 Bronson Rd. (Exit 20, I-95), is an early saltbox with wildflower & herb gardens. Adm.; open Thurs.—Sun., spring—fall.

GLASTONBURY

Glastonbury/Rocky Hill Ferry, rte. 160, has been in operation since 1655. Fare; crossings Wed.—Sun., spring—fall.

Holland Brook Audubon Center, 1361 Main St. (Exit 7, rte. 2), has a touch table plus weather corner; 38-acre park & trails adjacent to center. Free; closed Mon. 633-8402

Museum-On-the-Green, 1944 Main St. (Exit 9, rte. 2), displays Indian & early in-

dustrial artifacts. Donation; open Mon. & Thurs., spring—fall.

GREENWICH

Audubon Center, 613 Riversville Rd. (Exit 28, rte. 15), is a 485-acre sanctuary with 15 miles of trails; exhibits. Adm. 869-5272

Bruce Museum, Museum Dr. (Exit 3, I-95), has marine center focusing on animals of Long Island Sound, plus exhibits on Indian cultures. Adm.; closed Mon. 869-0376

Putnam Cottage (c. 1690), 243 E. Putnam Ave. (rte. 1), (Exit 5, I-95), was meeting place for Gen. Israel Putnam & other patriots; rare scalloped shingles, huge fireplaces. Kids under 12 free; Mon., Wed., Fri. or by appt. 869-9697

GROTON

Ebenezer Avery House (1750), Ft. Griswold, has weaving room & colonial kitchen; nearby park was where Benedict Arnold's British troops attacked Americans. Free; house open summer weekends, park year-round. 446-9257/-1529

Bluff Point SP, Depot Rd. off rte. 1, offers salt marshes, sand beach, rocky bluff, woods to explore.

River Queen Cruises, Thames Harbour Inn, Thames St., offers sightseeing cruises; fare. Runs spring—fall. 445-8111

USS *Nautilus* Memorial, US Naval Sub Base, rte. 12 (Exit 86, I-95), was world's first nuclear-powered sub; working periscopes, control room, mini-theaters, self-guided tour of *Nautilus*. Free; closed Tues. & major holidays. 449-3174/-3558

HADLYME

Gillette Castle SP, 67 River

Rd. off rte. 82 (Exit 6 or 7, rte. 9), has a medieval-style castle that was home of actor who played Sherlock Holmes. Adm.; open spring—fall. 526-2336

HAMDEN

Sleeping Giant SP, rte. 10, is named for a 2-mile mountain resembling a sleeping man; adm. on weekends.

☆ HARTFORD

Bushnell Park, Jewell St. (Capitol Area Exit, I-91; Exit 49, I-84), has an old-fashioned carousel. 728-3089

CT Hist. Soc., 1 Elizabeth St. (Exit 46, I-84), has changing exhibits. Adm.; closed Mon. & summer Sat. 236-5621

Deep River Navigation Co., Charter Oak Dock, near Regional Market, Brainard Rd., offers trips along waterfront & CT River. Fare; June—Oct. 526-4954

Museum of CT History, 231 Capitol Ave. in State Lib. (Cap. Area Exit, I-84), displays 1662 Royal Charter. Free; closed Sun. & holidays. 566-3056

Nook Farm, Farmington Ave. (Exit 46, I-84), has carefully restored homes of Harriet Beecher Stowe & Mark Twain. Adm.; open daily summer, closed Mon. rest of year. 525-9317

Old State House (1796), 800 Main St. (Exit 31, I-91; Exit 52, I-84), is a Bulfinch-designed building with Gilbert Stuart portrait of George Washington. Free; open daily. 522-6766

Red Rover Ltd., Old State House, offers sightseeing trips on double-decker buses. Fare; runs Tues.—Sat. year-round. 525-5155

Science Museum of CT, 950 Trout Brook Dr. (Exit 43, I-84), W. Hartford, is a compre-

hensive nature/technology museum with aquarium, discovery room, hands-on tank, mini-zoo, planetarium with daily shows, full-size whale model that kids can walk into. Adm.; closed major holidays. 236-2961

State Capitol, 210 Cap. Ave. (Cap. Ave. Exit, I-84), runs tours weekdays. Free; 240-0222

Travelers Tower, 1 Tower Sq., Main St., offers the best views of the city; tours in summer. Free; open daily. 277-2431

Wadsworth Atheneum, 600 Main St., (I-84/I-91 to Main St.), is a nationally-recognized art gallery with taped tours for children & extra earphones for Mom or Dad; exhibits for visually handicapped. Kids 12 & under free; closed Mon. & holidays. 278-2670

KENSINGTON

Hungerford Outdoor Center, 191 Farmington Ave. at rtes. 372 & 71 (Exit 35, I-84), has animals (both domesticated & indigenous), exhibits, gardens, pond, trails. Affiliated with New Britain Youth Museum (See New Britain). Free for preschoolers; open spring—fall. 827-9064

KENT

Kent Falls SP, rte. 7, 3 miles north of town, has impressive cascades.

Lake Waramaug SP, rte. 478, 5 miles north of New Preston, is a beautiful lake. Fee on weekends & holidays.

Macedonia Brook SP, off rte. 341, offers vistas of Catskills & Taconic Ranges.

Sloane-Stanley Museum & Kent Furnace, rte. 7, has log cabin, old tools, ruins of iron furnace, studio of artist/au-

thor Eric Sloane. Adm.; open spring—fall, Wed.—Sun. 927-3849/566-3005

LEDYARD

Nathan Lester House (1793), Vinegar Hill Rd. & Long Cove off Rte. 12, is typical of early farm here; museum & original outbuildings. Donations; open summer, Tues., Thurs. & weekends, or by appt. 464-0266

Sawmill, Iron St. (rte. 214), is a colonial up-and-down saw in an 11-acre park; blacksmith shop, shingle mill. Free; saw operates spring & fall. 464-8740/-2874

Stoddard Hill SP, rte. 12, 5 miles south of Norwich, offers wonderful views.

LITCHFIELD

Conservation Center, rte. 202, on White Memorial Foundation grounds, has self-guided trail & special displays, games, nature library for kids on state's largest preserve; horseback riding. Adm. to Center; hiking on trails is free. Center closed Mon., grounds open daily. 567-0015, Center; 567-0857, Foundation.

Mt. Tom SP, rte. 202, 3.5 miles west of Bantam, is a beautiful lake with stone tower for views. Fee; open daily.

MADISON

Hammonasset Beach SP, (Exit 62, I-95), offers 2 miles of beach with concessions. Fee for parking; open in summer. 245-2785

MANCHESTER

Fire Museum, 230 Pine St. (Exit 3, I-384), displays old-fashioned fire equipment. Donations; open spring—fall. 649-9436

Lutz Children's Museum, 247 S. Main St., rte. 83 (Exit 60, I-84; Exit 3, I-384), is a hands-on museum with live animals & kid-sized dinosaur model; outdoor play area, nearby nature center. Adm.; closed Mon. & holidays. 643-0949

Wickham Park, 1329 W. Middle Tpk. (Exit 60, I-84), has aviary, gardens, log cabin, playgrounds & ponds on 215 acres. Fee for parking; open spring—fall. 528-0856

MIDDLEBURY

Quassy Amusement Park, rte. 64 (Exit 16E/17W, I-84), is a 20-acre lakeside playground; concessions, free petting zoo. Fees for individual rides; open spring—fall. 758-2913

MYSTIC

Denison Pequotsepos Nature Center, Pequotsepos Rd. (Exit 90, I-95), is a 125-acre sanctuary with natural history museum & self-guided trails (one for the blind); 1717 homestead nearby (536-9248). Adm.; closed Mon. in winter. 536-1216

Mystic Marinelife Aquarium, Coogan Blvd. (Exit 90, I-95), has over 6,000 specimens in 45 exhibits plus indoor theater & outdoor Seal Island. Adm.; closed major holidays. 536-3323

Mystic Seaport Museum, rte. 27 (Exit 90, I-95), is a nationally acclaimed "living" history center; children's museum, craft demonstrations, cruises, planetarium in restored old buildings & authentic ships. Adm.; closed Christmas. 572-0711

Nearby **Olde Mistick Village** (536-4941) has shops, restaurants, Memory Lane Doll & Toy Museum; information center. 536-1641

NEW BRITAIN
Copernican Space Science Center, Central CT State Univ., 1615 Stanley St. (Exit 40, I-84), is an observatory plus planetarium with one of largest public telescopes in US; special shows for kids. Adm. 827-7419/-7852

New Britain Museum of American Art, 56 Lexington St. (Exit 35, I-84), has sizeable collection; many pieces by NE painters Copley, Sargent, Stuart, Whistler. Free; closed Mon. & holidays. 229-0257

New Britain Youth Museum, 30 High St., rte. 72 to Columbus Blvd., exhibits Americana, circus miniatures, dolls; many participatory programs. Affiliated with Hungerford Outdoor Center (See Kensington). Free; closed Sun. & Mon. 225-3020

NEW CANAAN
New Canaan Hist. Soc., 13 Oenoke Ridge (Exit 37, rte. 15), has several interesting old buildings plus costume collection. Kids free; openings vary. 966-1776

New Canaan Nature Center, 144 Oenoke Ridge, rte. 124, offers hiking trails on 40 acres of varied terrain, nature displays, solar greenhouse. Free; open daily. 966-9577

NEW HAVEN
Black Rock Fort & Fort Nathan Hale, Woodward Ave. (Exit 50, I-95), are reconstructed Rev. & Civil War forts with harbor views. Free; open daily in summer, weekends in fall. 787-8790

CT Children's Museum, 567 State St. (Exit 3, I-91), provides fantasy play & hands-on experience for young kids; parents encouraged to join in. Adm. 777-KIDS

East Rock Park, E. Rock Rd. (Willow St. Exit, I-91), has playground & trails in largest city park/bird sanctuary; views of harbor & Long Island Sound. Free; open daily. 787-6086

M/V *Liberty Belle*, Long Wharf Pier (Exit 46, I-95), cruises harbor; half-hour lunch trip ideal for preschoolers. Fare; spring—fall. 562-4163

Lighthouse Point Park, 2 Lighthouse Rd. (Exit 50, I-95), has a carousel, views of Long Island Sound. Adm., parking fee. 787-8005

Peabody Museum of Natural History, 170 Whitney Ave. (Exit 3, I-91), is NE's largest natural history display: dinosaurs, minerals, insects & shell collections; Discovery Room, hands-on experience, special kids' programs. Free on Tues.; closed major holidays. 432-5050/-5799

Picnic Performances, summer concerts in city parks. 787-8023

Schooner, Inc., 60 S. Water St., offers educational/ecological cruises aboard research ketch. Fare; spring—fall. 865-1737

West Rock Nature Center, Wintergreen Ave. (Exit 59, rte. 15), has native animals. Free; closed holidays. 787-8016

Eli Whitney Museum, Whitney Ave. & Armory St., 5 blocks from Peabody Museum, is best for mechanically-oriented older kids; focus on famous inventor's contribution to manufacturing. Free. 777-1833

Yale University, 344 College St. across from New Haven Green (Exit 47, I-95), offers hour-long tours of campus where Nathan Hale, William H. Taft, Noah Webster studied. Free; open daily. 432-2300

NEW LONDON
CT Arboretum, CT College, Williams St. (Exit 83S/84N, I-95), has 425 acres of shrubs & trees to explore. Free; open daily. 447-1911

Lyman Allyn Art Museum, 625 Williams St. (Exit 83, I-95), is small museum with dolls, toys, whaling captain's home. Donations; closed Mon. & holidays. 443-2545

Nathan Hale Schoolhouse (1774), Captain's Walk (Exit 83N/84S, I-95), is restored schoolhouse where Hale taught before enlisting in Rev. army. Open summer. 269-5752

Harkness Mem. SP, off rte. 213.

New London ferries combine convenience with sightseeing; fare (reservations advised if planning to take your car): Block Island auto ferry departs Ferry St. spring—fall (442-7891/-9553); Fishers Island auto ferries leave New London pier daily from foot of Captain's Walk, year-round (443-6851 or 516/788-7463); Orient Point LI auto ferry departs Ferry St. year-round (443-5281).

Ocean Beach Park, Ocean Ave. (Exit 82A northbound/83 southbound, I-95), is a seaside amusement park with rides & boardwalk. Adm., parking fee; open summer. 444-3031

Thames Science Center, Gallows Ln. off Williams St. (Exit 83, I-95), is a regional museum with changing exhibits & special programs about the river basin. 442-0391

US Coast Guard Academy, Mohegan Ave. (Exit 83, I-95), has multi-media show; training tall ship *Eagle* open weekends when in port. Free; open spring—fall. 444-8270

Ye Olde Town Mill, 8 Mill St. (Exit 83N/84S, I-95), is an overshot wheel. Free; grounds open year-round. 444-2206

NIANTIC
Millstone Energy Center, 278 Main St. (Exit 74, I-95), has exhibits, games, films. Free; open daily in summer, weekends rest of year. 447-1791

Rocky Neck SP, rte. 156 (Exit 72, I-95), is a mile-long crescent beach. Parking fee in summer. 739-5471

NORWALK
Lady Joan, Beach Rd., Cove Marina (Exit 16, I-95), is a replica paddlewheeler that cruises harbor & islands daily. Fare; runs summer only. 838-9003

The Maritime Center, 10 N. Water St. (Exit 14N/15S, I-95), has aquarium, IMAX theater, oyster house, wooden boat demonstrations. Adm.; open daily. 838-1488

NORWICH
Indian Burial Grounds, Sachem St. off rte. 32, is resting place of Uncas, Mohegan chief friendly with settlers.

Mohegan Park, Mohegan Rd. (Exit 81E, I-395), has recreational facilities & zoo. Open daily. 886-2381, ext. 210

Norwich River Cruises, City Pier, has a steel catamaran that offers close-ups of subs & US Coast Guard Academy. Fare; runs spring—fall. 535-2066

POMFRET
Brayton Grist Mill & Marcy Blacksmith Museum, Mashamoquet Brook SP, rte. 44. Free; open Thurs., Sat., Sun., summer only.

Mashamoquet Brook SP, rte. 44, 5 miles west of Putnam, offers variety of outdoor recreation; wolf den where Israel Putnam tracked down the animal preying on village livestock. Adm. on weekends & holidays; open year-round.

ROCKY HILL
Dinosaur SP, West. St. (Exit 23, I-91), has dinosaur tracks housed in giant geodesic dome; 40 acres of nature trails. Adm. (museum); closed Mon. 529-8423

SHARON
Housatonic Meadows SP, rte. 7, 1 mile north of Cornwall Bridge.

Northeast Audubon Center, rte. 4, is a large sanctuary with self-guided trails. Adm.; closed major holidays. 364-0520

SIMSBURY
Massacoh Plantation, 800 Hopmeadow St. (rte. 10), is a complex of buildings & exhibits representing 3 centuries of local history. Adm.; closed major holidays. 658-2500

Stratton Brook SP, rte. 305, 2 miles west of town, makes a shady retreat in hot weather. Adm.; open daily.

Talcott Mt. SP, rte. 185, offers 1-mile hike to tower with views of 4 states; local history museum. Open daily in summer; less often in fall. 677-0662

STAMFORD
Bartlett Arboretum, Univ. of CT, 151 Brookdale Rd. (Exit 35, rte. 15), has 63 acres of gardens & woodlands; swamp walk. Free; open daily. 322-6971

Stamford Museum & Nature Center, Scofieldtown Rd. (Exit 35, rte. 15), is an old working farm with animals & tools, country store, Indian & natural history displays, nature trail, planetarium. Adm.; closed major holidays. 322-1646

Whitney Museum of Am. Art, 1 Champion Plaza (Exit 7, I-95), is CT branch of prestigious NY gallery. Free; closed Sun. & Mon. 358-7603/-7652

STONINGTON

Clyde's Cider Mill, Stonington Rd. (Exit 90, I-95), is the last steam-powered cidermaker in NE. Free; operates weekend afternoons in fall. 536-3354

Maple Breeze Park, rte. 2 (Exit 92, I-95), Pawcatuck, is another amusement park with bumper boats, go-cart track, mini-golf, waterslide. Adm.; open in summer. 599-1232

Old Lighthouse Museum, 7 Water St., was first government-operated lighthouse in CT; fishing & whaling gear, toys, kids' room. Adm.; open spring—fall, closed Mon. 535-1440

STORRS

CT State Museum of Natural History, Univ. of CT, rte. 195 (Exit 68, I-84), displays birds of prey, fossils, Indian artifacts, minerals; "Great White Shark Exhibit." Free; open daily. 486-4460

Gurleyville Grist Mill, Stonemill Rd. (Exit 68, I-84), is stone mill museum. Donations; open Sun. only, spring—fall. 429-6526

Univ. of CT, Main Campus, rte. 195 (Exit 68, I-84), has animal & dairy barns, homemade ice cream; closed Easter & semester recess. 486-3530

STRATFORD

Am. Shakespeare Theatre, Elm St. (Exit 32, I-95),

is one of US' leading theaters. 375-5000

Boothe Mem. Park & Museum, Main St. (Exit 53, rte. 15), is a 32-acre farm with unusual, historic buildings; playground. Open spring—fall. 375-1233/378-9895

Judson House & Museum, 967 Academy Hill (Exit 32, I-95; Exit 53S, rte. 15), Putney, is a colonial home with slave cellar. Preschoolers free; open Wed., Sat., Sun., spring—fall. 378-0630

TERRYVILLE

Lock Museum of America, 130 Main St. (Exit 34, I-84), is largest collection in US; 22,000 locks & keys trace this industry from local beginnings. Kids free; open spring—fall. 589-6359

TORRINGTON

Burr Pond SP, rte. 8, 5 miles north of town, has scenic trail around site of Borden's first US condensed milk factory. Adm.; open daily.

Hotchkiss-Fyler House (1900), 192 Main St. (Exit 44, rte. 8), is Victorian home & museum. Closed Sun. 482-8260

John A. Minetto SP, rte. 272, 6 miles north of town.

WASHINGTON

Am. Indian Archaeological Institute, Curtis Rd. off rte. 199 (Exit 15, I-84), has Algonkian village, artifacts, longhouses, mastodon skeleton; craft workshops & films. Preschoolers free; open daily. 868-0518

WATERBURY

Mattatuck Museum, 194

W. Main St., chronicles the industrial history of "Brass City." Free; closed Mon., major holidays & Sat. July & Aug. 753-0381

WESTPORT

Nature Center for Envir. Activities, 10 Woodside Ln. (Exit 17, I-95; Exit 41, rte. 15), is a 62-acre sanctuary with museum (animal shelter, aquarium, science exhibits). Adm.; open daily. 227-7253

Sherwood Island SP, 2 miles south of I-95, Exit 18, has scuba diving facilities.

WETHERSFIELD

Buttolph-Williams House (c. 1692), Broad St. (Exit 26, I-91), has authentic early kitchen. Adm.; open spring—fall. 529-0460/-8996

WINDSOR

CT Fire & Trolley Museum, 58 North Rd. (rte. 140), (Exit 45, I-91), Warehouse Point, displays a century's worth of fire trucks; trolley rides. Adm.; open spring—fall. 623-4732/-6540

WINDSOR LOCKS

NE Air Museum, rte. 75, Bradley Int. Airport (Exit 40, I-91), has more than 80 aircraft, including helicopter model by CT inventor; flight simulator, films. Preschoolers free; closed major holidays. 623-3305

Area code: 401
For further information on state parks, call 277-2632.

ANTHONY

Greene Homestead (1770), 50 Taft St., was home to the famous general. Donations; open Wed., Sat. & Sun., or by appt. March—Nov. 821-8630

ARCADIA

Arcadia SP, rte. 165, has 13,000 acres to explore.

Dovecrest Trading Post & Indian Museum, Summit Rd., displays native artifacts & crafts; serves authentic Indian foods. Open daily. 539-7795

Tomaquag Indian Mem. Museum, Summit Rd., has Indian crafts including largest US display of ash-split baskets. Donations; by appt. 539-2094

BLOCK ISLAND offers

exciting fishing; its water may be among the best in the world for cod, flounder, swordfish, or tuna:

Block Island Beach is an 18-acre recreation area.

Ferries run from Galilee year-round; fees. Navigation Co., Galilee State Pier, Point Judith 02882. In summer, there are also ferries from Newport, Providence & New London. 789-3502 or 421-4050

BRISTOL

Blithewold Gardens & Arboretum, rte. 114 to Ferry Rd., has self-guided walk, 82' giant sequoia on a turn-of-the-century estate. Preschoolers free; grounds open daily year-round, tours Tues.—Sun., mid-April—Oct. 253-2707

Colt SP has nature program, horseback riding. 253-7482

Ferries run to Hog & Prudence Islands, Church St. Wharf. Fee; open spring—fall.

Haffenreffer Museum of Anthropology, near rte. 136 & Tower Rd., has 400 acres of woodland, including site where Puritans met with RI Indians. Preschoolers free; open at various times year-round. 253-8388

CHARLESTOWN

Breachway, rte. 1 & Charlestown Breach Rd.

Burlingame SP, rte. 1, 5 miles west of town, is state's largest recreation area.

Chamber of Commerce hosts an annual seafood festival in Aug. 364-3878

Charlestown Hist. Soc., Old Post Rd. (rte. 1A) on Cross Mills Lib. grounds, is 19th-century schoolhouse. Open Wed. & Sat. or by appt. 364-7507

Indian Burial Ground, Narrow Ln. off rte. 1, is resting place of Narragansetts.

Indian Church, off rte. 2, welcomes visitors Sun.

Kimball Wildlife Refuge, rte. 1 onto Montauk Rd. to signs, is state Audubon sanctuary with exhibits & programs for kids. Parking fee; open daily.

Ninigret Park, off rte. 1A, has 174 acres with spring-fed swimming pond; nature center with trails, 10-speed bike course.

DIAMOND HILL

Diamond Hill SP, rte. 114, 1 mile north of town, offers winter & summer activities.

EAST GREENWICH

Goodard SP, Ives Rd., has golf & horseback riding.

James Mitchell Varnum House (1773), was home to RI general. Adm.; open Tues.—Sat. in summer, closed holidays. 884-4622

HOPE VALLEY

Enchanted Forest, rte. 3 (Exit 2, I-95), has farm animals, fire engine, nature trail plus amusements & rides with storybook theme. Adm.; open spring—fall. 539-7711

JAMESTOWN

Beavertail SP, by lighthouse, has naturalist on duty in summer; 1938 hurricane uncovered early colonial stonework on US' third lighthouse. Park open Wed.—Sun. in summer. 423-9920

Fire Dept. Mem. Bldg., Narragansett Ave., exhibits 1885 steam engine & other antique equipment. Open weekdays. 423-0062

Jamestown Museum, Narragansett Ave., displays ferry memorabilia. Donations; open in summer, closed Sun. & Mon.

Philomenian Lib., North Rd., has prehistoric Indian artifacts & exhibits on early settlers of Conanicut Island. Free; closed weekends. 423-2665

Prospect Hill, off Beavertail Rd., offers views plus Rev. War earthworks.

Watson Farm (c. 1796), North Rd., is a 280-acre working farm. Donations; tours of grounds Tues., Thurs., Sun. 277-3956

Windmill (1787), North Rd. off rte. 138, is open in summer on weekends. Donations. 423-1798

LITTLE COMPTON
RI Red Monument, rtes. 81 & 179, Adamsville, honors state bird.

Wilbor House (1680), rte. 77 at W. Main Rd., exhibits carriages, sleighs & old schoolhouse. Adm.; open Tues.—Sat. in summer. 635-4559

MIDDLETOWN
Norman Bird Sanctuary, 3rd Beach Rd., has cliffs, fields, swamps; museum with natural history display, special programs. Kids under 13 free with adult; closed major holidays. 846-2577

Prescott Farm, rte. 114, has country store, museum with Pilgrim artifacts, working windmill. Adm.; open daily April—Dec. 847-6230

Purgatory Chasm, Easton Point off Purgatory Rd., is narrow cleft in rocks with scenic overlook.

NARRAGANSETT
Canonchet Farm/South County Museum, rte. 1A across from bathhouses, is 174-acre park; fitness course & small working farm (open daily). Museum exhibits artifacts of early RI settlements. Preschoolers free;

open Wed.—Sun. in summer, weekends rest of year. 783-5400

Narragansett Towers, Ocean Rd., rte. 1A, are all that remain of Stanford White-designed casino.

Scarborough Beach, Ocean Rd., 2 miles north of Point Judith.

Roger W. Wheeler Beach, Sand Hill Cove Rd., has 27 acres in Galilee.

NEWPORT
Beechwood Mansion, 580 Bellevue Ave., was Astors' summer "cottage"; costumed actors recreate the splendor of Newport's gilded era, fun for older kids. Adm.; open daily June—Oct. 846-3772

Cliff Walk, Mem. Blvd., is a famous path right at the ocean's edge (hold young kids' hands); views of Newport's mansions, including the Vanderbilts' Chinese teahouse.

Fort Adams SP, rte. 114 to Ocean Dr., offers sailboat rentals (849-8385) & beach (847-2400); Museum of Yachting on grounds (adm.; open summer—fall, 847-1018). Fee for park; open summer only.

Hammersmith Farm, next to Fort Adams on Ocean Drive, runs 45-minute tours of the estate where John Kennedy married Jackie; miniature horses. Adm.; open spring—fall. 846-0420

King's Park gives fine views of the harbor & Ida Lewis Yacht Club.

Int. Tennis Hall of Fame, Newport Casino, 194 Bellevue Ave., may interest older kids who take the game seriously. Adm.; open year-round. 849-3990

Newport Art Museum, 76 Bellevue Ave., displays paintings in 1862 Richard

Morris Hunt mansion. Kids free; closed holidays. 847-0179

Newport Hist. Soc., 82 Touro St., is museum with ship models, recreated merchant's parlor. Kids under 12 free; open various times year-round. 846-0813

Old Colony & Newport RR, America's Cup Ave., offers 40-minute trips to Portsmouth on 1930s train. Fare; open summer. 624-6951

Oldport Harbor Tours, Newport Yachting Center, America's Cup Ave., runs hour-long narrated cruises. Fare; open summer & fall. 849-2111

Old Stone Mill, Bellevue Ave. & Mill St., was built by Norsemen or early colonists.

Redwood Lib. & Athenaeum (1747), 50 Bellevue Ave., has collection of early Am. paintings, including some of Gilbert Stuart's work. Free; closed Sun. & holidays. 847-0292

Touro Synagogue Nat. Hist. Site, 85 Touro St., is oldest such place of worship in US; interior is architectural masterpiece. Closed Sat. & holy days except for services. 847-4794

Trinity Church (1726), Queen Anne Sq., has Handel organ & regular concerts. Free; open daily in summer & fall, or by appt. 846-0660

Wanton-Lyman-Hazard House (1675), 17 Broadway, was site of Stamp Act Riot; Jacobean architecture with working colonial kitchen & garden. Kids under 12 free; open Tues.—Sat. in summer. 846-0813

PAWTUCKET
Children's Museum of RI, 58 Walcott St. (Exit 28 or 29, I-95), has puzzle room, play

firehouse, puppetry; Grandmother's Kitchen & room-sized relief map of state in 1840 mansion, special events. Adm.; open various times year-round. 726-2590

Slater Mill Hist. Site, Roosevelt Ave. (Exit 28, I-95), demonstrates hand-spinning at Slater's water-powered mill; canal, dam, riverside park plus 90-min. tours (best for older kids). Adm.; varying schedule spring—fall. 725-8638

Slater Park, Newport Ave., has carousel & zoo; summer concerts Sun.

PORTSMOUTH, once the biggest town in the colony, was founded by Anne Hutchinson:

Founders Mem. Grove, across from Founders Brook off Boyd's Ln., is open daily.

Green Animals Topiary Gardens, Cory's Ln. off rte. 114, has 80 trees & shrubs sculpted into animals, birds, or people; small toy museum. Adm.; open daily spring—fall. 847-1000

Old Schoolhouse, E. Main St. & Union St., is said to be the nation's oldest. Open weekend afternoons in summer, or by appt. 683-3858

☆ PROVIDENCE

Brown University, College Hill at end of College St., offers tours during academic year. 863-2378

Lincoln Woods SP, rte. 146, 5 miles north of city, is large recreation area; horseback riding.

Museum of Art, RI School of Design, 224 Benefit St., has extensive collections, including Am. painting & furniture. Donations on Sat.; open year-round except Mon. & holidays. 331-3511

Museum of RI History, 110 Benevolent St., exhibits changing displays of state history in Federal-style home. Adm.; closed Mon. & holidays. 331-8575

Old Market Bldg., Market Sq., commemorates Providence Tea Party & hurricane of 1815.

Pawtucket Red Sox, McCoy Stadium, Columbus Ave. (Exit 2A, I-95S; Exit 28, I-95N), is the farm team that produced Ellis Burks & Mike Greenwell; free youth clinics in summer. Adm.; open spring & summer. 724-7303

State House, Smith St. between Francis & Gaspee, has first unsupported marble dome in US & a portrait of Washington by Stuart. Free; closed weekends & holidays. 277-2311

Roger Williams Nat. Mem., 282 N. Main St., has visitor center on site of original settlement. Free; open daily spring—fall, closed weekends rest of year. 528-5385

Roger Williams Park, Broad St. & Park Ave. (Elmwood Ave. Exit, I-95), has amphitheater for concerts, aviary, kids' rides, zoo; Betsy Williams Cottage (1773) & Museum of Natural History (closed Mon. & holidays). Free; park open daily. 785-9450

SAUNDERSTOWN/ SOUTH KINGSTOWN

Casey Farm (c. 1750), rte. 1A, is an unspoiled, early farm. Preschoolers free; open Tues., Thurs. & Sat. afternoons. 508/227-3956

East Matunuck SP, rte. 1, 3 miles southeast of Perryville, has over 100 acres to explore.

Goose Nest Spring Hatch-ery, Hatchery Rd. off rte. 4, Lafayette, is open daily. 294-4662

Great Swamp Monument, off rte. 2, marks the end of King Philip's War.

Perryville Trout Hatchery, 2426 Post Rd., is open daily. 783-5358

Gilbert Stuart Birthplace, Gilbert Stuart Rd., 1 mile off rte. 1, is 1750 snuff mill. Adm.; open spring—fall, Sat.—Thurs. 294-3001

Univ. of RI has a fossils & minerals collection on the first floor of Green Hall. 792-2265

Washington Cty. Jail, 1348 Kingstown Rd., contains old cells; period rooms & garden. Open Tues., Thurs. & Sat. afternoons. 783-1328

TIVERTON

Fort Barton, Highland Rd., is Rev. War redoubt with trails & views. Free; open year-round.

Ruecker Wildlife Refuge, Seapowet Ave., is an Audubon sanctuary with trails. Open daily. 624-2759

WARREN

Bay Queen Cruises, 461 Water St., Gate 4, offers 6-hr. narrated cruises of Narragansett Bay with stopovers in Newport. Fare; runs spring—fall. 245-1350

Firemen's Museum, 42 Baker St., displays 1802 engine in Victorian building. By appt. 245-7600

WARWICK recreates the burning of the *Gaspee* in mid-June:

City Beach, Asylum Rd., has 170 acres to explore.

Conimicut Point, east off rte. 117, is a good place to dig for quahogs.

Oakland Beach, Oakland Beach Ave. south of rte. 117.

Rocky Point Park, rte. 117, Warwick Neck, offers family recreation; carousel, games, rides. Adm.; open spring & summer. 737-8000

Warwick Museum, Kentish Artillery Armory, 3259 Post Rd., exhibits local history year-round. Adm.; closed Mon.

WEST GLOCESTER

George Washington SP, rte. 44, 2 miles east of town, offers Nordic skiing in winter.

WESTERLY

Babcock-Smith House (c. 1732) was town's first post office; Georgian home of early physician. Adm.; open Wed. & Sun. in summer. 598-4424

Flying Horse Carousel (c. 1867), Bay St., Watch Hill, is the oldest of its kind (horses suspended from center pole; centrifugal force makes them fly out). For kids only; open summer.

Misquamicut Beach, rte. 1A, 5 miles south of town, is popular with surfers.

Wilcox Park, High St. near Merchants Sq. parking, has smell-taste-touch garden for handicapped on 18 acres. 348-8362

WICKFORD

Smith's Castle (c. 1678), rte. 1, was originally plantation & trading post, believed to be the only home remaining in RI that Roger Williams visited. Adm.; open Thurs.—Sun. or by appt. 294-3521

MASSACHUSETTS

For information on state parks (unless otherwise noted), call 617/727-3180.

ACTON
Children's Discovery Museum, 177 Main St., has hands-on exhibits on science, music, nature & art; special displays on dinosaurs & the ocean, discovery ship. Adm.; closed Mon. 508/264-4200

AMHERST
Pratt Museum of Natural History, on Amherst College campus, off rte. 9, has fossils, skeletons, geologic exhibits. Free; open when school is in session, closed holidays. 413/542-2165

ASHLEY FALLS
Bartholomew's Cobble, off rte. 7A, 1/2 mile west of town on Weatogue Rd., is 227-acre nature preserve on Housatonic River; natural history museum. Adm.; open daily spring—fall.

ATTLEBORO
Capron Park, rte. 123, 1 mile west of town, is zoo with rain forests. Free; open daily year-round. 508/222-3047
Attleboro Museum Center for the Arts, 199 County & Dennis Sts., has art & history exhibits. Free; closed Mon. & month of Aug. 508/222/2644

BARNSTABLE
Donald G. Trayser Museum, on rte. 6A in Old Customs House, displays ship models, nautical equipment & paintings. Adm.; open Tues.—Sat. in summer.

BECKET
Jacob's Pillow Dance Festival, George Carter Rd. off rte. 20E, hosts performances by major dance groups. Adm.; open mid-June—early Sept. 413/243-0745 (information), 800/223-1814 (tickets).

BELCHERTOWN
Charles L. McLaughlin Trout Hatchery, off rte. 9, raises rainbow, brown & brook trout. Free; open daily. 413/323-7671

BEVERLY
Balch House Museum (1636), 448 Cabot St., is one of the oldest frame houses in US; period furnishings. Adm.; open Wed.—Sat., mid-May—mid-Oct. 508/922-7076
Cabot House Museum (1781), 117 Cabot St., has textile display & items pertaining to Continental Navy. Adm.; open same hours as Balch House. 508/922-1186
Chamber of Commerce, 303 Cabot St., offers self-guided driving tour brochures of historic houses & points of interest. Open Mon.—Fri. 508/922-1451
John Hale House Museum (1694), 39 Hale St., contains witchcraft artifacts. Adm.; open same hours as Balch House. 508/922-1186
Le Grand David & His Own Spectacular Magic Co., Cabot St. (rte. 22 exit, rte. 128), has afternoon & evening shows for kids; preschoolers happiest sitting in front. Adm.; open year-round. 508/927-3677
Sedgwick Gardens at Long Hill Reservation, 572 Essex St. (Exit 18, rte. 128N), offers 114 acres of trails; labeled trees & flowers on estate grounds. Kids free; open daily. 508/922-1536

☆BOSTON
Area code: 617

By foot:
Boston by Foot, starting at Samuel Adams statue, Congress St. near Faneuil Hall, offers guided tours, "Heart of Freedom Trail." Fee; leaves at various times, May—Oct. 367-2345
Boston by Little Feet, conducts guided tours for children 8-12 (& adult friends) on Sun. p.m. (See Boston by Foot.)
Freedom Trail is self-guided tour beginning at information kiosk on Tremont St. side of Boston Common. Park Rangers also lead tours (free) from visitor center, 15 State St. Red line on pavement leads past both State Houses, Nat. Park Service Visitor Center, site of Boston Massacre, Faneuil Hall, Paul Revere House, *USS Constitution*, Bunker Hill Monument & more.
Harborwalk is mile-long tour along wharves from Old State House to Boston Tea Party Ship, where shuttle bus returns participants to starting point. Walking tour brochures available from Boston Common Visitor Center, NE Aquarium, Children's Museum & Boston Tea Party Ship.

Bus & Trolley Tours:
Boston Tours (899-1454),
Boston Trolley Tours
(427-TOUR), **Old Town
Trolley** (269-7010) lets kids
ride free with adult, & **Hub
Bus Lines** (739-0100) has
double-decker buses.

*Cruises of Boston Harbor
operate in summer:*
MA Bay Lines (at Rowes
Wharf, 542-8000 or 749-
4500), **Boston Harbor
Cruises** (at Long Wharf,
227-4321) & **Bay State
Provincetown Cruises** (at
Long Wharf, 723-7800).

Charles River Cruise:
Skyline Cruises, Inc. (at
dock behind Museum of
Science) operates mid-
May—Sept. 523-2169

Arnold Arboretum,
Arborway in Jamaica Plain,
has 14,000-specimen collection of plants & trees in 125-
acre botanical garden. Free;
open daily. 524-1718
Boston Nat. Hist. Park
includes 7 sites along
Freedom Trail; visitor
center, 15 State St., has
films & exhibits. Free; open
daily. 542-5642
**Boston Tea Party Ship &
Museum,** at Congress St.
Bridge, is full-scale replica
recreating colonists' famous
protest against taxation
without representation;
audiovisuals, tea served.
Adm.; open daily. 338-1773
Bunker Hill Monument,
Breed's Hill in Charlestown,
has 221' obelisk on site of
Rev. War battle; dioramas &
model of battle. Free; open
daily. 242-5641
**Charles River Reserva-
tion** is 961-acre park
extending on both sides of
the river from Boston to

Newton Upper Falls; 6
swimming pools, golf course,
tennis courts, jogging paths,
Boston Pops esplanade
concerts in summer. Free;
open daily.
Charlestown Navy Yard,
off rte. 1 in Charlestown,
displays *USS Constitution*
("Old Ironsides") & destroyer
in 30-acre park. Free guided
tours of *Constitution* (242-
5670). Park museum (242-
7400) has maritime exhibits;
free. Constitution Museum
(426-1812) offers participa-
tion in running a colonial
ship; model shipbuilding
demonstrations; adm. All
exhibits closed on major
winter holidays.
**Children's Museum of
Boston,** next to Tea Party
Ship east of Congress St.
Bridge, offers wide variety of
hands-on exhibits, including
sculpture to climb, TV
newsroom with closed circuit
monitors, manhole leading
to a tunnel, factory assembly
line, supermarket & dental
office. Adm. except Fri. eve.;
closed Sun. except in summer & major winter holi-
days. 426-8855
**Christian Science Pub-
lishing Soc.,** MA Ave. &
Norway St., has hollow globe
of world that can be walked
through. Free; closed major
winter holidays; 450-3790.
Multimedia Bible Exhibit
has nondenominational
audiovisual programs, time-
line, children's corner. Free;
closed Tues. & major winter
holidays.
Computer Museum, next
to Tea Party Ship, 300
Congress St., tells story of
information revolution
through hands-on exhibits &
video programs. Adm.; open
daily in summer, Tues.—
Sun. rest of year; closed
major winter holidays. 423-

6758
Faneuil Hall, in Faneuil
Hall Marketplace, was
gathering place for Rev. War
patriots; paintings of battles
& military museum. Free;
building open daily. Museum
open Mon.—Fri.; 523-2980.
Marketplace includes
restored Quincy Market, a
lively collection of boutiques,
restaurants, free outdoor
entertainment.
Fenway Park, near
Kenmore Sq., presents
always-interesting Boston
Red Sox in animated atmos-
phere. Bleachers offer least-
expensive opportunity to rub
elbows with loyal NE fans.
267-1700
Fort Warren, on Georges
Island in Boston Harbor,
was used in 4 wars; accessible by ferry from Long
Wharf (see Bay State
Cruises above).
**John Hancock Observa-
tory,** Copley Sq., has
glassed-in deck, telescopes &
audiovisual programs with
overview of past & present
Boston. Adm.; closed
Thanksgiving & Christmas.
247-1976
**Museum at John F.
Kennedy Library,** Colum-
bia Point in Dorchester (Exit
15S or 14N, Southeast
Expressway), examines life
& times of the president
through exhibits & audiovisual presentations. Kids
under 16 free; open daily
except major winter holi-
days. 929-4523
Museum of Fine Arts, 465
Huntington Ave., is a re-
nowned collection of paintings, furniture, sculpture,
crafts & relics from around
the world; drop-in workshop
& gallery programs for kids
6-12. Kids under 16 free;
open Tues.—Sun. except
major holidays. 267-9300

Museum of Science, at Charles River Dam Bridge, offers many hands-on exhibits & interpretive programs for all ages. Omni Theater with 4-story domed screen & popular planetarium require separate fee. Adm.; open Tues.—Sun. except Thanksgiving & Christmas. 523-6664

New Charles River Dam Information Center, Charles River in Charlestown, has brief multimedia presentation describing locks, fish ladder, flood control; guided tours. Free; open daily. 727-0059

NE Aquarium, Central Wharf, off Atlantic Ave., is a major Boston attraction; nose-to-nose viewing of 2,000 fish; daily dolphin & sea lion performances, penguin exhibit, tide-pool touch tank, films. Adm.; closed Thanksgiving & Christmas. 742-8870

NE Sports Museum, 1175 Soldiers Field Rd., traces area athletics through memorabilia & audiovisuals. Adm.; open Thurs.—Sun. except Christmas & New Year's. 254-2299

Old North Church, 193 Salem St. in North End, is site of famous "one if by land...two if by sea" signal. Free; open daily. 523-6676

Old South Meeting House, 310 Washington St., held many important pre-Revolutionary meetings; multimedia presentation & scale model of city interpret colonial times. Adm.; closed major winter holidays. 482-6439

Old State House (1713), State & Washington Sts., is Boston's oldest public building; exhibits 3 centuries of artifacts. Free to MA students; closed major holidays. 242-5655

Paul Revere House, 19 North Sq. in North End, is city's oldest home. Adm.; closed Mon. (Jan.—mid-April) & major winter holidays. 523-2338

Prudential Center, between Huntington Ave. & Boylston St., offers fantastic view of the city & surrounding countryside from 50th-floor Skywalk. Adm.; open daily. 236-3318

Public Garden, next to Boston Common, is the heart of this city. Paved walkways circle the pond made famous by *Make Way for Ducklings*; swan boat rides (fee; run spring—mid-Sept.). Park free; open daily.

State House, Beacon at Park St., has guided tours of historic Bulfinch-designed building. Free; open Mon.—Fri. 727-3676

Where's Boston, 100 Huntington Ave., in USA Cinema at Copley Place Mall, is a 50-min. film presentation of Boston. Adm.; closed Thanksgiving & Christmas. 267-4949

BOURNE

Aptucxet Trading Post Museum, Canal Bridge on Shore Rd., 1 mile south of town, is replica of 1627 trading post with Pilgrim, Dutch & Indian relics; runestone from 1000 A.D., saltworks, windmill, herb garden, Grover Cleveland's private RR station, guided tours. Adm.; open daily in summer, hours vary spring & fall, closed in winter. 508/759-9571

BRAINTREE

Gen. Sylvanus Thayer Birthplace, 786 Washington St., exhibits crafts, furnishings, Civil War memorabilia; barn with sleighs, tools, icehouse equipment, costumes. Adm.; open Tues., Thurs.—Sun., spring—fall; weekends only rest of year. 617/848-1640

BREWSTER

Cape Cod Museum of Natural Hist., rte. 6A, 1 1/2 miles west of town, displays native flora & fauna; nature trails. Adm.; open daily in summer, closed Mon. & holidays rest of year. 508/896-3867

Drummer Boy Museum, rte. 6A, 2 miles west of town, exhibits life-size 3-D paintings of Rev. War. Adm.; open daily mid-May—mid-Oct. 508/896-3823

NE Fire & Hist. Museum, rte. 6A, exhibits early fire equipment; diorama of Chicago fire, apothecary shop, herb garden, blacksmith shop. Adm.; open daily in summer, weekends only in fall. 508/896-5711

Nickerson SP, rte. 6A, has ample campsites; interpretive program. 508/896-3491

Old Gristmill, Stoney Brook Rd., off rte. 6A, is on site of early gristmill. Free; open Wed., Fri., Sat. in summer.

Sealand of Cape Cod, rte. 6A, 3 miles west of town, has aquariums, seal pool, sea lion lagoon, performing dolphins. Adm.; open daily in summer; hours vary rest of year. 508/385-9252

BROOKLINE

John F. Kennedy Nat. Hist. Site, 83 Beals St., is birthplace of our 35th president. Kids free; open daily except major holidays. 617/566-7937

Museum of Transportation, 15 Newton St. in Larz Anderson Park, exhibits carriages & automobiles from 1899 to 1968. Adm.; open Wed.—Sun., mid-May—early Oct. 617/522-6140

CAMBRIDGE
Cambridge Discovery information booth at Harvard Sq. sells tour maps.
Hart Nautical Galleries, at MA Institute of Technology (M.I.T.), 55 MA Ave., displays ship & engine models that trace history of marine engineering. Free; open daily.
Harvard Information Center, 1350 MA Ave., gives free tours of oldest university in US. Tours Mon.—Sat. when school is in session. 617/495-1573
Harvard Univ. Museums of Natural History, 24 Oxford St. & 11 Divinity Ave., consist of 4 museums: Peabody (archeology), Geological & Mineralogical, Botanical (700 glass flowers) & Comparative Zoology (fossils, fish & reptiles). Free Sat. a.m.; closed Mon. 617/495-1910
Longfellow Nat. Hist. Site, 105 Brattle St., was poet's home; Geo. Washington's headquarters in 1775-76. Free garden concert series in Sept. Kids under 12 free; open daily except major holidays. 617/876-4491
M.I.T. offers guided tours of its 135-acre campus from the Information Center, 77 MA Ave. Free; Mon.—Fri. 617/253-1000

CAPE COD (Also see listings under towns of Barnstable, Brewster, Chatham, Eastham, Falmouth, Hyannis, Provincetown, Sandwich, S. Wellfleet & W. Yarmouth):

Cape Cod Nat. Seashore, HQ on rte. 6 at Marconi Station, S. Wellfleet, has 28,000 acres of dunes, beaches, ponds, marshes, woods & cliffs on the outer Cape. 2 visitor centers, extensive interpretive programs; trails for biking & hiking; guided walks & lectures April—Nov. Parking fee in summer; open year-round. 508/349-3785

CHARLEMONT
Mohawk Trail State Forest, rte. 2, is well-developed reserve on 6,500 acres, interpretive program. Fee; open daily year-round. 413/339-5504

CHATHAM
Chatham RR Museum, Depot St., is former railroad station with model trains & telegraph equipment. Donations; open weekdays in summer.
Gristmill, off Shattuck Pl., is wind-powered. Free; open daily in summer, closed Tues.

CONCORD
Concord Museum, Cambridge Tpk. & Lexington Rd., chronicles town's history in 15 period rooms; exhibits artifacts of Emerson & Thoreau, lantern that signaled Paul Revere's ride. Adm.; open daily except major holidays. 508/369-9609
Great Meadows Nat. Wildlife Refuge, rte. 62, 1 1/2 miles east of town, offers interpretive nature trails through marshes & along Concord River. Free; open daily. 508/443-4661
Minute Man Nat. Hist. Park, rte. 2A, is spread over Concord, Lexington &

Lincoln. 2 visitor centers with well-designed interpretive programs bring the events of 1775 into focus: Battle Rd. Visitor Center, Exit 30, I-95/rte. 128, serves as starting point & shows 22-min. film. Free; open daily April—Nov. 617/862-7753. North Bridge Visitor Center, Concord, displays military uniforms & equipment; formal gardens overlooking North Bridge. Free; open daily. 508/369-6944 or 617/484-6156 (from Boston area)
The Old Manse, Monument St., was home to Emerson & Hawthorne at different times. Adm.; guided tours Thurs.—Mon. & holidays. 508/369-3909
Orchard House, Lexington Rd., was home to Louisa May Alcott, author of *Little Women*. Adm.; open daily April—mid-Sept., hours vary rest of year. 508/369-4118
Walden Pond, rte. 126, has replica of cabin Thoreau built. Parking fee.

DALTON
Crane Museum of Papermaking, rte. 9, in the Old Stone Mill, traces history of papermaking. Crane & Co. makes paper used in currency. Free; open Mon.—Fri., June—mid-Oct. 413/684-2600
Wahconah Falls SP, off rte. 9, is near scenic waterfall. 413/442-8992

DUXBURY
Alden House (1653), Alden St., was last home of John & Priscilla Alden. Adm.; open in summer, closed Mon. 617/934-6001
Myles Standish Monument, Crescent St., commemorates the town's founder.

EASTHAM
Old Windmill, rte. 6, near town hall, is oldest on Cape; occasionally grinds corn. Free; open daily in summer.

EASTHAMPTON
Arcadia Wildlife Sanctuary, Ft. Hill Rd., off East St. from rte. 5 (Exit 10, I-91), offers self-guided trail network & visitor center with greenhouse; MA Audubon programs throughout year. Adm.; sanctuary closed Mon., visitor center closed Sun. & Mon., both open holidays. 413/584-3009

FALL RIVER
Battleship Cove, Exit 5, I-95, has mothballed Navy ships open for inspection; Marine Museum traces history of steam transportation. Adm.; open daily except major holidays. 508/678-1100

Fall River Heritage SP, next to Battleship Cove, displays city's textile & nautical history in visitor center; boardwalk along waterfront. Fee for boats only; closed Mon. & major holidays. 508/675-5759

FALMOUTH
Ashumet Holly Reservation & Wildlife Sanctuary, off Ashumet Rd., is Audubon-operated holly collection & bird sanctuary on 45 acres; barn swallow colony in summer. Adm.; open daily May—Oct. 508/563-6390

FRAMINGHAM
Danforth Museum of Art, 123 Union Ave., consists of 6 fine arts galleries including special children's gallery. Donations; open Tues.—Sun. except holidays. 508/620-0050

Garden in the Woods, Hemenway Rd. off Raymond Rd., 8 miles west of town on rte. 20, has the largest collection of wildflowers in Northeast; self-guided tours on 45 acres. Adm.; open mid-April—Oct., closed Mon. 508/877-6574

GARDNER
Gardner Heritage SP, 1 mile north of rte. 2, has visitor center with exhibits & videos on chairmaking industry. Free; open year-round, closed major holidays & Mon. Nov.—April. 508/630-1497

GLOUCESTER
Cape Ann Whale Watch/ Gloucester Sightseeing Cruises, Rose's Wharf, offers narrated whale watches & cruises around harbor. Fee; both cruises run daily in summer; whale watches also Fri. & Sat. in spring & fall. 508/283-5110

Daunty Fishing Fleet, Rose's Wharf, narrates cruise around Cape Ann & harbor; lobstering demonstrations in canopied boat. Fee; departs daily in summer, weekends spring & fall. 508/283-5110

Fishermen's Memorial, Western Ave. on the harbor, is statue dedicated to fishermen lost at sea.

Good Harbor Beach, rte. 127A, is popular for its excellent surf. Parking fee; open daily in summer. 508/283-1601

Hammond Castle Museum, Hesperus Ave. south of town, is medieval-style castle on a cliff overlooking the bay; occasional concerts on 8,000-pipe organ. Adm.; open daily in summer, Thurs.—Sun. rest of year, closed major holidays. 508/283-2080

Seven Seas Whale Watch, Seven Seas Wharf at Gloucester House Restaurant, offers narrated whale watches & harbor cruises. Fee; departs daily May—Oct. 508/283-1776

Stage Fort Park, on Gloucester Harbor, has small beach, playground, trails, free summer concerts. Parking fee; beach open daily in summer (lifeguards), park open year-round.

Whale Safaris, Gateway Marina, on Crafts Rd., offers narrated whale watches. Fee; departs daily, spring—fall. 508/281-4163

GOSHEN
DAR State Forest, East St., is popular day-use park on 1,500 acres.

GREAT BARRINGTON
Monument Mt. Reservation, off rte. 7, 4 miles north of town, has panoramic views from 1,642' summit; open daily.

Mt. Everett State Reservation, near S. Egremont in town of Mt. Washington, offers views of three states. Fee; closed to automobiles in winter.

Albert Schweitzer Center, Hulbert Rd., off rte. 7 via Taconic Ave. & Alford Rd., exhibits memorabilia of famous humanitarian; children's garden, Philosopher's Walk & wildlife sanctuary. Donations; grounds open daily, center closed Mon. 413/528-3124

HADLEY
Hadley Farm Museum, on rte. 9 next to town hall, displays stagecoach, wagons, oxcarts, farm implements. Free; open daily except Mon., May—mid-Oct.

HAMPDEN

Laughing Brook Education Center & Wildlife Sanctuary, 789 Main St., was home of children's author Thornton W. Burgess (also see Sandwich); 5 miles of trails (one for visually impaired), NE animals in enclosures, greenhouse, nature & environmental exhibits. Adm.; open Tues.—Sun. & Mon. holidays. 413/566-8034

HANCOCK

Jiminy Peak Alpine Slide, off rte. 43, 1/2 mile east of town, offers chair lift, alpine slide, miniature golf, fishing. Adm.; open daily in summer, weekends in spring & fall. 413/738-5500

HARVARD

Fruitlands Museums, Prospect Hill Rd., was home of Bronson Alcott. Museums include: 18th-century farmhouse with period furnishings, Shaker House, American Indian Museum, Picture Gallery. Adm.; grounds open daily year-round, museums open Tues.—Sun., mid-May—mid-Oct. 508/456-3924

HINGHAM

The Old Ordinary (1680), Lincoln St., displays period furnishings & toys in 13 rooms. Adm.; open Tues.—Sat. in summer.
Old Ship Meetinghouse (1681), Main St., is a good example of a colonial church. Open Tues.—Sat. in summer. 617/749-1679
Wompatuck SP, Union St., has 2,877 acres; interpretive program. 617/749-7160

HOLYOKE

Children's Museum, 444 Dwight St., offers hands-on exhibits, including firehouse, post office, TV station, papermill & print shop. Adm.; open Tues.—Sun. 413/536-4637

Holyoke Heritage SP, behind City Hall, has multimedia program & guided walks of city's canals & mills; rides on antique railroad cars mid-May—mid-Oct. Fee for rides, park free; open daily. 413/534-1723

Mt. Tom, rte. 141 (Exit 17W, I-91), has 20 miles of trails; playground & nature museum. Fee; museum open in summer, park open year-round. 413/527-4805
Wistariahurst, near the corner of Cabot & Beech Sts., is Victorian home of a wealthy silk manufacturer. Mansion can be explored freely; youth museum with exhibits on local wildlife & Native Americans, dinosaur tracks. Donations; closed Mon. 413/534-2216

HYANNIS

Cape Cod & Hyannis RR, at east end of Main St., offers narrated rides on restored coaches to Sandwich, Buzzard's Bay & Falmouth with connections from Boston, Brockton & Middleboro; optional boat trips to Martha's Vineyard, Cape Cod Canal & Hyannis Harbor. Train can be boarded at any station. Fare; runs mid-May—Oct. 508/771-1145
Hyannis Harbor Tours, Pier 1 at Ocean St. dock, has sightseeing tours of harbor, with views of the Kennedy compound. Fare; runs daily spring—fall. 508/775-7185
Hyannis Whale Watcher Cruises, from Iyanough Hills Motor Lodge, rte. 132, with shuttle buses to Barnstable Harbor, offers narrated cruises. Fare; departs daily spring—fall. 508/775-1622 or 362-6088
Hy-Line Cruises, Pier 1 at Ocean St., runs to Martha's Vineyard & Nantucket. Fare; departs daily spring—fall. 508/775-7185
Melody Tent, W. Main St., offers musicals & children's shows. Adm.; performances nightly with matinees Thurs. & Sat. in summer. 508/775-9100

IPSWICH

Castle Hill, Argilla Rd., holds concerts & art lectures on summer weekends. Adm. 508/356-4070
Cranes' Beach, end of Argilla Rd., has 4 miles of superb beaches & sand dunes; parking fee. Open daily in summer.
Goodale Orchards, Argilla Rd., is an apple orchard/farm/produce shop; farm animals, cider mill operation, tractor-drawn hayrides, well-equipped sand pile. Berry picking mid-June—mid-Aug. Free; open mid-June—Christmas Eve. 508/356-5366

LAWRENCE

Lawrence Heritage SP, 1 Jackson St., chronicles the history of mills at visitor center (restored workers' boarding house); walking tours along canals Sat. a.m. Free; open daily spring—fall, closed Mon. rest of year. 508/794-1655

LENOX

Pleasant Valley Wildlife Sanctuary, W. Dugway Rd., off rtes. 7/20, features beaver pond, hummingbird garden, limestone cobble, 7 miles of trails, museum with nature exhibits & Audubon interpretive program; guided walks & lectures. Adm.; open daily, closed Mon. & major winter holidays. 413/637-0320

Tanglewood, Hawthorne Rd., is summer home of the Boston Symphony Orchestra; Berkshire Music Festival July & Aug. Adm. 413/637-1940

LEXINGTON

Visitor Center, next to Buckman Tavern opposite the Common, is a good starting point. Open daily. **Hist. Soc.** opens Buckman Tavern (617/861-0928), Hancock-Clarke House (36 Hancock St., 862-5598) & Munroe Tavern (1322 MA Ave., 862-1703) — all from Rev. War period. Adm.; open mid-April—Oct.

Lexington Battle Green (the Common), MA Ave. & Bedford St., is site of the first skirmish in Rev. War; famous Minuteman statue at east end.

Minute Man Nat. Hist. Park, see listing under Concord.

Museum of Our Nat. Heritage, 33 Marrett Rd., features exhibits on famous Americans. Free; closed major winter holidays. 617/861-6559

Old Belfry, off Clarke St. near the Common, is a reproduction of the bell sounded to assemble the Minutemen.

LINCOLN

DeCordova Museum/ Dana Museum & Park, Sandy Pond Rd. (Exit 28B, I-95), is a castle-like structure in 35-acre woodland setting. Exhibits 20th-century art, mainly by NE artists; outdoor sculpture park; summer concerts. Adm.; closed Mon. & holidays. 617/259-8355

Drumlin Farm Education Center & Wildlife Sanctuary, S. Great Rd. (rte. 117), is home to MA Audubon Society. Trails through fields & woodland; farm animals in barns & native fauna in special live exhibits. Several family programs, including winter & spring vacation-week activities. Adm.; closed Mon. & winter holidays. 617/259-9807

LOWELL

Lowell Nat. Hist. Park & Heritage SP, 246 Market St. (Visitor Center), focuses on massive textile mills. Guided walking tours of mills & canals; barge & trolley tour. Waterpower exhibit has hands-on models of waterwheels; slide show & museum shop at visitor center. Free, including tours; closed major winter holidays. 508/459-1000

MARTHA'S VINEYARD

Felix Neck Wildlife Sanctuary, off Edgartown-Vineyard Haven Rd., offers 200 acres of dunes, marsh, reptile pond & beach; Audubon-run visitor center has exhibits, crippled raptor rehabilitation barn, waterfowl-rearing program. Adm.; open daily. 508/627-4850

Windfarm Museum, Edgartown Rd., is a petting farm & open-air museum; tours of windmills & pumps, solar- & wind-powered farmhouse. Adm.; open Thurs.—Tues. in summer. 508/693-3658

MILTON

Blue Hills Reservation, south end of Blue Hills Pkwy., has 300 miles of trails & bridle paths. Beach, tennis courts & golf course in summer; ice skating.

Blue Hills Trailside Museum, rte. 138 (Exit 2B, I-93), offers Audubon-operated museum with nature & Indian exhibits; local fauna in outdoor exhibits. Active interpretive program for families. Adm.; closed Mon. & major winter holidays. 617/333-0690

NANTUCKET ISLAND

Maria Mitchell Science Center, 1 Vestal St., is restored birthplace of famous astronomer. Adm.; open Tues.—Sat. in summer. 508/228-2896

Museum of Natural Science, 7 Milk St., exhibits native wildflowers & birds. Adm.; open Tues.—Sat. in summer (508/228-0898). Observatory open Wed. nights in summer (508/228-9273).

Nantucket Hist. Assn., Broad St., operates 11 properties; Foulger Museum chronicles island history, exhibits on farming, crafts, Indians & Quakers. Adm.; open daily year-round. Whaling Museum displays items related to island's most important industry. Adm.; open daily, June—mid-Oct. 508/228-1894

NATICK

Broadmoor Wildlife Sanctuary, rte. 16, 2 miles west of town, consists of 600 acres of varied habitat along the Charles River; visitor center in restored barn, active interpretive programs for all ages. Adm.; open Tues.—Sun. 508/655-2296 or 617/235-3929

NEW BEDFORD

New Bedford Fire Museum, Bedford & Sixth Sts.,

exhibits old engines & uniforms; rides offered on occasion. Kids under 12 free; open daily in summer. 508/992-2162

Whaling Museum, 18 Johnny Cake Hill, displays whaling relics, humpback whale skeleton, half model of whaling bark to board; film in summer. Adm.; closed major winter holidays. 508/997-0046

NEWBURYPORT

Chamber of Commerce, 29 State St., has walking tour brochures of High St. area.

Custom House Maritime Museum, 25 Water St., has exhibits on Coast Guard & maritime history; audiovisual program gives an overview of port. Adm.; open daily mid-March—Dec., Mon.—Fri. rest of year.

Parker River Nat. Wildlife Refuge, Plum Island, offers 6 miles of superb beach; 4,600 acres of dunes & salt marsh, major stopover for migrating birds (many trails, observation lookouts & boardwalks). Adm.; open daily. 508/465-5753

NORFOLK

Stony Brook Nature Center & Wildlife Sanctuary, North St., off rte. 115, 2 miles north of intersection with rte. 1A, includes mile-long trail to boardwalk over marsh, butterfly garden; extensive interpretive programs in nature center. Donations; open Tues.—Sun. 508/528-3140

NORTH ADAMS

Natural Bridge SP, rte. 8, 1 1/2 miles north of town, features marble natural bridge & chasm; tours &

interpretive programs. Adm.; open daily June—mid-Oct. 413/663-6312

Western Gateway Heritage Park, Furnace St., offers railroading exhibits in 6 restored buildings. Mini-train rides; tours on summer & fall weekends. Free; closed major winter holidays & Jan. 15-31. 413/663-6312

NORTHAMPTON

Look Mem. Park, rte. 9 on northwest edge of town, is well-developed 200-acre park with swimming pool, tennis courts & miniature railroad. Fee for recreational facilities; open daily in summer.

NORTH ANDOVER

Museum of American Textile Hist., 800 MA Ave., traces development of wool industry & Industrial Rev.; weaving demonstrations; tours (except Sun.). Adm.; closed Mon. & holidays. 508/686-0191

NORTHFIELD

Northfield Mt. Recreation & Environmental Center, rte. 63, 7 miles south of town, offers a variety of hands-on activities; tour of hydroelectric dam on CT River. Bus tour of reservoir explains dams & dikes; tour of powerhouse (kids must be 12 & older). Free; center & tours Wed.—Sun., closed a week in spring & fall. 413/659-3714

Cabot Station Fishway, rte. 2, Turners Falls, is a series of fishladders for spawning salmon & shad; viewing windows. Free; fish migrate May & June. 413/659-3714

Northfield Mt. has well-marked nature & hiking trails; snowshoeing instruc-

tion & rentals.

 Quinnetukut II, Riverview Picnic Area, rte. 63 across from Northfield Mt. Visitor Center, runs narrated cruise of CT River in a canopied boat. Adm.; departs daily June—mid-Oct. (reservations advised). 413/659-3714

NORTH MIDDLEBORO

A&D Toy Train Village & RR Museum, 49 Plymouth St., 2 miles north of rtes. 18/28/44, displays over 2,000 trains, many operating. Adm.; closed major holidays. 508/947-5303

ONSET

Cape Cod Canal Cruises, Town Pier, runs narrated tours of Canal. Fee; departs daily June—mid-Oct., weekends in May. 508/295-3883

PITTSFIELD

Berkshire Museum, South St., has paintings, natural history dioramas, aquarium, films. Free; open daily in summer, closed Mon. rest of year. 413/443-7171

Berkshire Public Theater, 30 Union St., offers a wide range of performances with children's shows. Adm.; open daily (reservations). 413/445-4631

Canoe Meadows Wildlife Sanctuary, Holmes Rd. off rte. 7 (Exit 2, I-90), is a 242-acre tract along the Housatonic River; Audubon programs, 3 miles of trails. Adm.; open Tues.—Sun. 413/637-0320

Hancock Shaker Village, rte. 20, 5 miles west of town, consists of 20 restored buildings, including a round stone barn; active interpretive program. Adm.; open daily June—Oct. 413/443-0188

PLYMOUTH

Capt. John Boats, Town Wharf, runs whale-watching cruises. Fee; departs daily in summer, weekends spring & fall. 508/746-2643

Cranberry World, 225 Water St., displays working bogs & harvesting equipment; cooking demonstrations 4 times daily, samples. Free; open daily April—Nov. 508/747-1000

Jenny Gristmill, Spring Ln. in Town Brook Park, is a working reproduction of Plymouth Colony's first mill; interpretive program, duck feeding encouraged. Open daily April—Dec., closed Mon. rest of year. 508/747-0811

Mayflower II, State Pier, has costumed guides to describe life during the Pilgrims' voyage. Adm.; open daily April—Nov. 508/746-1622

Pilgrim Hall Museum, Court & Chilton Sts. (rte. 3A), displays personal items of Pilgrims, remains of the *Sparrow Hawk* (1626). Adm.; closed Christmas & New Year's. 508/746-1620

Plimouth Plantation, rte. 3A, 3 miles south of town, is a realistic living history museum (costumed "residents" know nothing of the world after 1627). Adm.; open daily April—Nov. 508/746-1622

Plymouth & Provincetown Steamship Co., State Pier, connects the South Shore with the Cape; harbor cruises & whale watching en route. Fee; cruises daily in summer, weekends in May, runs to Provincetown daily year-round. 508/747-2400

Plymouth Nat. Wax Museum, 16 Carver St., chronicles Pilgrim history with life-size displays. Adm.; open daily March—Nov. 508/746-6468

PRINCETON

Wachusett Meadow Wildlife Sanctuary, Goodnow Rd. off rte. 62, is a 900-acre tract with many wildlife environments; interpretive stations along Audubon trails. Adm.; open Tues.—Sun. 508/464-2712

Wachusett Mt. State Reservation, Mountain Rd., has trails open summer & winter. Fee for downhill skiing. 508/464-2987

PROVINCETOWN

Dolphin Fleet, MacMillan Pier, runs 9 whale-watching trips daily mid-April—Oct.; fee. 508/255-3857 or 800/826-9300

Pilgrim Monument, off rte. 6 on Town Hill, offers views of town & harbor from 252' tower; museum with ship models, whaling equipment, relics from shipwrecks & *Mayflower* memorabilia. Adm.; open daily April—Nov. 508/487-1310

Portuguese Princess Whale Watch, MacMillan Pier, has naturalist-conducted whale watches. Fee; departs daily April—Nov. 508/487-2651 or 800/442-3188

Provincetown Heritage Museum, Commercial & Center Sts., has art & environmental displays; antique firefighting equipment. Kids under 12 free; open daily June—mid-Oct. 508/487-0666

Provincetown Whale-Watch Cruises, MacMillan Pier, runs naturalist-conducted whale watches. Fee; departs daily mid-April—mid-Oct. 508/487-

1582 or 800/992-9333

ROCKPORT

Halibut Point SP, Granite St., sits on a rocky promontory jutting into the Atlantic; interpretive program, walking trails. Fee; open year-round. 508/546-2997

Paper House, off rte. 127 at Pigeon Cove, was built & furnished with newspapers. Small adm.; open daily in summer.

SALEM

Chamber of Commerce, Old Town Hall on Front St., has walking tours of historic port. 508/744-0004

Essex Institute Museum Neighborhood, 132-4 Essex St., displays furnishings and memorabilia of 3 centuries in several houses & museum. Adm.; museum open daily June—Oct., closed Mon. rest of year & major winter holidays. 508/744-3390

House of Seven Gables, 54 Turner St., gives tours of 4 buildings, including Nathaniel Hawthorne's birthplace. Adm.; closed major winter holidays & end of Jan. 508/744-0991

Peabody Museum of Salem, 161 Essex St., has maritime & natural history exhibits. Adm.; open daily except major winter holidays. 508/745-9500

Pier Transit Co. Cruises depart from 2 locations: Salem Willows Amusement Park Pier & Central Wharf on Derby St.; Salem Harbor sightseeing tours & whale watches. Fee; daily departures for both in summer; harbor tour departs weekends only May, June & Sept. 508/744-6311 or 745-1208

Salem Maritime Nat. Hist. Site, on Derby St. waterfront, is restoration of the old port of Salem; tours start at

Custom House. Free; open daily, buildings closed major winter holidays. 508/744-4323

Salem Witch Museum, 19 1/2 Washington Sq. N., depicts witch trials; audio-visual presentation. Adm.; closed major winter holidays. 508/744-1692

SALISBURY BEACH

Salisbury Beach State Reservation, Beach Rd., off rte. 1, is MA's northernmost beach; one of few camp-grounds in area. 508/462-4481

SANDWICH

Green Briar Nature Center, 6 Discovery Hill Rd., focuses on naturalist Thornton W. Burgess, author of *Peter Rabbit*; Old Briar Patch Trail is mile-long nature walk, active interpretive program. Free tours of Green Briar Jam Kitchen, where jams & jellies are made (demonstrations Mon.—Fri.). Donations; trail open daily, nature center, kitchen & gift shop open daily May—Dec., shop open Thurs.—Sat. rest of year. 508/888-6870

Heritage Plantation, Grove & Pine Sts., off rte. 6A, consists of 6 buildings on 76 acres with wide array of Americana: arts, crafts, antique military firearms, restored automobiles plus gardens, trails & mill; jitney tours available. Adm.; open daily, mid-May—mid-Oct. 508/888-3300

Scusset Beach State Reservation, Scusset Beach Rd., offers various activities; adm. 508/888-0859

Thornton W. Burgess Museum, 4 Water St., has mementos of Burgess' life. Donations; closed Easter,

Thanksgiving & Christmas. 508/888-4668

Yesteryears Doll & Miniature Museum, River & Main Sts., displays dolls & dollhouses Adm.; open daily, mid-May—Oct. 508/888-1711

SAUGUS

Saugus Ironworks Nat. Hist. Site, 244 Central St., has blast furnace, water-wheel, forge; film & black-smith demonstrations. Guided tours April—Oct. Free; closed Thanksgiving & Christmas. 617-233-0050

SHARON

Kendall Whaling Museum, Everett St., displays outfitted whaleboat & items pertaining to whaling; Arctic exhibit. Adm.; open Tues.—Sat., & Mon. holidays. 617/784-5642

Moose Hill Wildlife Sanctuary, Moose Hill St., off rte. 27E, offers family activities in MA Audubon sanctuary. Adm.; closed Mon. 617/784-5691

SOUTH CARVER

Edaville RR, rte. 58, runs 5 1/2 miles through cranberry bogs & recreated 19th-century shopping village; museum with railway items, antique automobiles, fire engine. Adm.; open daily in summer, hours vary rest of year. 508/866-4526

Myles Standish State Forest, Cranberry Rd., offers family activities on 14,000 acres; 475 campsites. 508/866-2526

SOUTH DARTMOUTH

Children's Museum of Dartmouth, 276 Gulf Rd., has hands-on exhibits, nature trails & picnic areas. Adm.; open daily, except ma-

jor holidays. 508/993-3361

SOUTH WELLFLEET

Wellfleet Bay Wildlife Sanctuary, rte. 6, 5 miles south of town, offers nature programs on scenic 700 acres; 5 miles of trails. Adm.; closed Mon. 508/349-2615

SPRINGFIELD

Forest Park, rte. 83, is a well-equipped urban park on 750 acres; miniature train rides, Kiddieland Zoo, paddle boats. Adm. to zoo, park free; closed major winter holidays. 413/787-6440

Naismith Mem. Basketball Hall of Fame, 1150 W. Columbus Ave. (Exits 4 & 7, I-91), lets visitors shoot baskets from moving walk-way; audiovisual presentations. Adm.; closed major winter holidays. 413/781-5759

Springfield Science Museum, Chestnut & State Sts., has dinosaur exhibit, aquarium, observatory, planetarium, hands-on exhibits; active interpretive program. Free, except planetarium show; closed Mon. & major winter holidays. 413/733-1194

STOCKBRIDGE

Norman Rockwell Museum, Main St. at Elm, is a permanent display of popu-lar artist's paintings. Adm.; closed major winter holidays & last 2 weeks of Jan. 413/298-3822

STONEHAM

Walter D. Stone Memorial Zoo, 149 Pond St., off rte. 28, displays animals in glass-fronted & moated enclosures; free-flight aviary. Adm.; closed Christ-mas & New Year's. 617/438-3662

STURBRIDGE
Cheney Orchards, off rte. 20, in Brimfield, has semi-dwarf trees for young apple pickers; antique fire engine rides on weekends during picking season. Free, except for fruit; apple season Sept.—mid-Oct. 413/245-9223

Old Sturbridge Village, rte. 20 (Exit 2, I-84 or Exit 9, I-90), recreates 1830's in NE; costumed interpreters perform daily chores in this 200-acre living history museum (40 buildings with 3 mills, guided tours, audiovisual programs, hands-on activities, special seasonal events). Adm.; closed Mon. Dec.—March plus Christmas & New Year's Day. 508/347-5383/-3362

Wells SP, Mountain Rd., has campsites on first-come-first-served basis, swimming (lifeguard) for campers only; interpretive programs, 5 miles of hiking trails. Adm. 508/347-9257

SUDBURY
Longfellow's Wayside Inn, rte. 20, 3 miles west of town, is restoration of famous old inn; includes museum (closed Christmas), gristmill, chapel (open April—Nov.) & schoolhouse (open May—Oct.). Kids under 12 free in restoration. 508/443-8846

TOPSFIELD
Ipswich River Wildlife Sanctuary, rte. 97, 1/2 mile east of rte. 1, is largest MA Audubon sanctuary with 10 miles of trails on 2,000 acres; rookery, observation tower, guided river float trips (reservations), canoe & cabin rentals, camping on island. Adm.; closed Mon.

508/887-9264

WALES
**Norcross Wildlife Sanctuary**, west of rte. 19 & east of rte. 32, offers 2 museums & trails on 3,000 acres. Free; closed Sun. & holidays. 413/267-9654

WESTFIELD
Stanley Park & Carillon, Western & Kensington Aves., has gardens, large inlaid slate map of N. America, covered bridge, mill, blacksmith shop; carillon concerts Thurs. & Sat. evenings & Sun. p.m., summer. Free; open May—mid-Oct.

WEST SPRINGFIELD
Storrowton Village Museum (1767-1834), rte. 147, 1 mile west of rte. 5, has restored buildings; tours in summer or by appt. Adm. to buildings, grounds free. 413/787-0136

WEST YARMOUTH
Aqua Circus, rte. 28, has dolphin & sea lion show, petting zoo, pony rides (summer only). Adm.; open daily mid-Feb.—Thanksgiving. 508/775-8883

WOODS HOLE
Nat. Marine Fisheries Service Aquarium, Water & Albatross Sts., is a major government research center with hands-on tank, seal pool, ship models, microscopic samples. Free; open daily in summer, Mon.—Fri. rest of year. 508/548-7684

WORCESTER
NE Science Center, rte. 9 east of town, is 60-acre park with indoor/outdoor zoo; railroad. Adm.; closed Mon., Tues. & major winter holidays. 508/791-9211

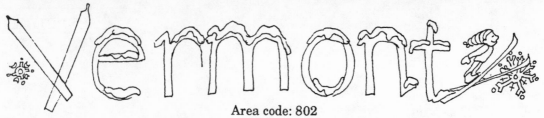

Vermont

Area code: 802
For information on state parks, call 244-8711.

Appalachian Trail Conference, PO Box 807, Harpers Ferry, WV 25424, has detailed descriptions & maps in *Appalachian Trail Guide to New Hampshire & Vermont.* 304/535-6331

The Connecticut River Watershed Council, 312 First NH Bank Building, Lebanon, NH 03766, gives up-to-date information on river conditions for canoeists. 603/488-2792

For a listing of day & residential camps for kids, write VT Camping Assoc., PO Box 133, Fairlee, VT 05045; free.

ARLINGTON
Battenkill Canoe Ltd., rte. 313, W. Arlington, has rentals & self-guided (some inn-to-inn) canoe tours; fee. 375-9559

Candle Mill Village, Old Mill Rd. off E. Arlington Rd., is a complex of shops in 3 old buildings; waterfall & rock ledges nearby are fun for kids. 375-2839

Norman Rockwell Exhibition, Main St., displays more than 1,000 *Sat. Eve.Post* covers & illustrations, many modeled on the locals; film. Kids under 12 free. 372-6423

ASCUTNEY
Ascutney Mt. Resort, rte. 44 (Exit 8 or 9, I-91), Brownsville, offers family fun year-round. 800/243-0011 or 484-7711

Ascutney SP, rte. 5 to Back Mountain Rd. (Exit 8, I-91), Windsor, has toll road up one of VT's few monadnocks.

676-2060
Old Constitution House, 16 N. Main St., Windsor, is where 6-day convention to adopt state constitution was held; former tavern with unusual concentrations of interesting early buildings nearby. Free; open daily spring—fall. 828-3226

VT State Craft Center, Main St., Windsor, has program of craft classes for kids; open year-round. 674-6729

Wilgus SP, Town Rd., 3 miles north of rte. 30 & Town Rd., offers recreation on CT River. 674-5422

BARNARD
Silver Lake SP, Town Rd., rents canoes; playground. 234-9451

BARRE
Rock of Ages, rte. 14, Graniteville (Exit 6, I-89), gives tours of large quarry in "granite center of the world"; visitor center. Free (except for train tours); open spring—fall. 476-3115

BELLOWS FALLS
Adams Old Stone Gristmill Museum, Mill St., is working mill with original equipment. Donations; open July & Aug. p.m. 463-3706

Green Mt. Flyer, One Depot Sq., runs sightseeing trips to Chester on 1935 vintage trains. Preschoolers free; spring & fall. 463-3069

BENNINGTON
Bennington Battle Monument, rtes. 9 & 7, commemorates decisive conflict

in Am. Rev.; views from tower, diorama & exhibits. Adm.; open daily spring—fall. 447-0550

Bennington Museum, W. Main St., has largest collection of renowned local pottery, also dolls, 1776 flag, luxury car built in town, Grandma Moses paintings, uniforms; Schoolhouse Museum. Adm.; open daily spring—fall. 447-1571

Burying Ground, Old First Church, Monument Ave., contains graves of VT's founders & poet Robert Frost; church is among most beautiful in NE. Donations (church); open in summer only (church).

Chamber of Commerce, Veterans Mem. Dr., offers free self-guided walking tour. 447-3311 or 442-4545

Fairdale Farm, 2 miles west of rtes. 7 & 9, is a good place for city kids to see what happens to milk before it is bottled. Free; open mid-May—mid-Oct. 442-6391

 Lake Shaftsbury SP, rte. 7A, Shaftsbury. 375-9978

Peter Matteson Tavern, East Rd., Shaftsbury, is a living-history museum; hands-on activities including churning butter, candle dipping, open-hearth cooking, workshops. 447-1571

Park-McCullough House, West. St., is a 35-room mansion; carriages & sleighs, tricycle in form of sulky & racehorse, playhouse replica of main house. Adm.; open summer & fall. 442-5441

Southern VT Orchards, rte. 7, 1 1/2 miles south of

town, has cidermaking demonstrations; windows for viewing baking. Free; open mid-Aug—Dec. 447-0714

Woodford SP, rte. 9, rents boats (not power). 447-7169

BETHEL

White River Nat. Fish Hatchery, rte. 107, displays work restoring Atlantic salmon; visitor center. Free; open daily. 234-5241

BRANDON

Branbury SP, rte. 7 to rte. 53, offers spectacular views of Lake Dunmore; nature museum, naturalist. 247-5925

Country Inns Along the Trail rents bikes; maps for self-guided tours. 247-3300

BRATTLEBORO

Brattleboro Museum & Art Center, Main & Vernon Sts., off rte. I-91 on rte. 5, displays changing art & hist. exhibits in 1915 railroad station; Estey organs. Donation; open p.m. April—Dec., except holidays. 257-0124

CT River Safari, Putney Rd., rte. 5, rents canoes, conducts inn-to-inn tours. 257-5008

Dummerston Maple Sugarhouse, Hickin's Mt. Mowings Farm, Black Mt. Rd., taps 2,000 trees a year; tours during sugaring season. 254-2146

Fort Dummer SP, Main St. & Old Guildford Rd. (Exit 1, I-91), has playground. 254-2610

BROOKFIELD

Floating Bridge is unique treat for all ages; closed in winter.

BURLINGTON

Ethan Allen Homestead, rte. 127, offers guided tours of simple home & farm in 286-acre park (free; open daily); historic tavern, periodic crafts demonstrations. Adm.; open mid-April—Oct. 865-4556

Battery Park, foot of Pearl St., has scenic views & free summer concerts; open daily.

Lake Champlain Ferries, King St. Dock, carries cars & passengers year-round to NY; fare. 864-9804

Spirit of Ethan Allen, Perkins Pier, narrates cruises along lake. Fare; open May—Oct. 862-8300

CABOT

Cabot Creamery, center of town, is a working cheese plant with self-guided tours, best in morning. Free; closed major holidays. 563-2231

CALAIS

Kent Museum, Kent's Corner, focuses on changes that shaped lives of Vermonters in 19th & early 20th centuries; barn, home, store. Archeology workshops, craft demonstrations; special events. Kids free with adult; open Thurs.—Sun. in July & Aug., weekends in foliage season. 828-2291 or 223-5660

Outdoor Tours Unlimited, Maple Corner, runs guided & self-guided canoe tours. 229-4570

CASTLETON

Hubbardton Battlefield & Museum, 7 miles north of rte. 4, E. Hubbardton, is site of only Rev. battle on VT soil; diorama & relief map. Free; open summer to mid-Oct. 828-3226

CHARLOTTE

Charlotte Mem. Museum, Museum Rd. east of rte. 7, displays locally-made Indian baskets, early household items. Free; open July & Aug. p.m. 425-2237

Lake Champlain Ferries (see Burlington) crosses here as well.

 VT Wildflower Farm, rte. 7, is 6 acres of field & woodland flowers; audiovisuals & self-guided tours. Kids under 13 free; open May—mid-Oct. 425-3500

ENOSBURG FALLS

Chester A. Arthur Birthplace, off rte. 36, N. Fairfield, is a simple clapboard home near the brick church where president's father preached.

 Lake Carmi SP, rte. 105 to rte. 236, has playground. 933-8383

ESSEX JUNCTION

Champlain Valley Exposition is held for a week around Labor Day.

 Discovery Museum, 51 Park St., is hands-on museum with art, history & science exhibits; facility for injured & orphaned wildlife, trail. Adm.; open various times year-round. 878-8687

 Underhill SP, rte. 15 to Town Rd., has trails up Mt. Mansfield. 899-3022

EAST DORSET

Emerald Lake SP, rte. 7, has marked trails, naturalist; playground. 362-1655

FAIR HAVEN

Bomoseen SP, rte. 4 to W. Shore Rd., has close to 3,000 acres to explore. 265-4242

 Half Moon SP, rte. 30 to Town Rd., 2 miles west then

1 1/2 miles south, has trails to High Pond. 273-2848

FERRISBURG
Kingsland Bay SP, Slang Rd., is on Lake Champlain. 877-3445

Mt. Philo SP, rtes. 7 & 22A, 6 miles north on rte. 7 to local road, 1 mile east, offers panoramic views. 425-2390

Rokeby Museum, rte. 7, was home to author/illustrator/naturalist & stop on underground railroad, "Hidden Room" housed runaway slaves; farm complex with outbuildings & garden. Preschoolers free; tours summer & fall, by appt. rest of year. 877-3406

GLOVER
Auger's Sugarmill Farm, rte. 16 south of Barton, uses woodburning evaporator to turn sap into syrup; Maple Museum. 525-3701

The Bread & Puppet Theatre Museum, rte. 122 off rte. 16, has hundreds of puppets in an old barn; tours, workshops. Free; open May—Oct. 525-6972 or 525-3031

GRAFTON
Grafton Hist. Soc. Museum, Main St., exhibits artifacts from local industries, old firefighting equipment, inkwells, photos, tools. Open Memorial—Columbus Day. 843-2344

Grafton Natural Hist. Museum, 2nd floor in Town Hall, displays Indian artifacts, fossils, minerals; field trips. Free; open Wed. p.m. (for kids) & Sat. p.m.

GRAND ISLE
Grand Isle SP, rte. 2, 5 miles north of S. Hero, has

fitness trail, naturalist on duty. 372-4300

Hyde Log Cabin, main road, is oldest building of its kind in US. Donations; open July—Labor Day. 828-3226

Knight Point SP, rte. 2 (Exit 17, I-89), N. Hero, is on Lake Champlain. 372-8389

GROTON
Boulder Beach, rte. 232 to Boulder Beach Rd., is open only for day use. 584-3823

Groton Nature Center, rte. 232 to Boulder Beach Rd., has guided activities, films, walks. 584-3827

Kettle Pond, rte. 232, offers group & winter camping only. 584-3820 or 584-3822

Osmore Pond, rte. 232, is accessible through New Discovery Campground. 584-3820 or 828-2454

Owl's Head, rte. 232, is mountain with scenic views.

Ricker Campground, rte. 232, has nature center, naturalist. 584-3821

Seyon Fly Fishing Area, rte. 302 to Town Rd., 3 miles west, is open May—Oct. 584-3829 or 828-2454

Stillwater Campground, rte. 232, is on Lake Groton. 584-3822

GUILDHALL
Maidstone SP, rte. 102 to State Forest Hwy., has naturalist on duty; salmon & trout fishing. 676-3930

HUNTINGTON
Birds of VT Museum, Sherman Hollow Rd., is a "museum in progress"; wood carvings & dioramas. Open daily (but suggest calling first). 434-2167

Camel's Hump SP, Huntington Center, has over

16,000 acres of scenic trails (alpine vegetation on summit), including Long Trail; one of few undeveloped peaks left in VT.

Green Mt. Audubon Nature Center, Richmond-Huntington Rd., has self-guided sugar-bush trail; variety of wildlife & 5 miles of trails.

JAMAICA
Jamaica SP, Town Rd., 1/2 mile north of Inn, has scenic trail to Hamilton Falls, naturalist; playground. 874-4600

West River Canoe, rte. 100, W. Jamaica, rents canoes. 896-6209

JAY
Jay Peak Aerial Tramway, off rte. 242, offers spectacular views into Canada summer or winter; fare. 988-2611

KILLINGTON
Gifford Woods SP, rte. 100, is on Kent Pond. 775-5354

Killington Resort, rte. 4 in Calvin Coolidge State Forest, is summer & winter resort; hour-long gondola rides. Fare; runs July—Oct. plus ski season. 422-3333

Pico Alpine Slide, rte. 4, has 2 slides & chairlift. Adm.; open June—mid-Oct. 775-4345

LUDLOW
Camp Plymouth SP, off rte. 100, offers a chance to pan for gold. 228-2025

Crowley Cheese Factory, rte. 103 to Healdsville Rd., then 2 miles west, is century-old factory; cheesemaking by hand (11:30-2:30 best time to watch). Free; closed holidays. 259-2340

Cycle-Inn-VT rents bikes; tours (some inn-to-inn) & maps. 228-8799/-8834

Green Mt. Sugar House, rte. 100, offers free samples. 228-7151

MANCHESTER
Am. Museum of Fly Fishing, rte. 7A & Seminary Ave., exhibits equipment of famous anglers, including Winslow Homer & Daniel Webster. Donation; open year-round. 362-3300

Bromley Alpine Slide, rte. 11, offers scenic views of 5 states; chairlift climbs to 4,882', summer concerts. Adm.; open summer—mid-Oct. & ski season. 824-5522

Hildene, rte. 7A, is 24-room Georgian Revival mansion, summer home to President Lincoln's son & descendants; visitor center, gardens with views, carriage barn. Adm.; open spring—fall & ski season. 362-1788

Mt. Equinox, rte. 7A, 5 miles south of rte. 11, is highest point in Taconics, views of NE, NY & Canada; auto road (cars need good brakes). Adm.; open spring—fall. 362-1114

MARLBORO
Marlboro Music Festival; July & Aug.

Luman Nelson Museum of NE Wildlife, rte. 9, Hogback Mt., displays 1,000 birds & animals year-round. 464-5494

MIDDLEBURY
Bicycle Holidays has rentals & self-guided tours. 388-2457

Chamber of Commerce, 35 Court St., provides walking-tour maps. 388-7579

Green Mt. Nat. Forest Ranger Station has guides & maps.

Sheldon Museum, 1 Park St., displays carpenter's shop, clocks, dolls, toys in 1829 brick home. Adm.; open summer & fall. 388-2117

UVM Morgan Horse Farm, rte. 125 to Weybridge St., rte. 23, breeds & trains "Figure's" descendants; tours, audiovisuals. Kids under 12 free; open spring—fall. 388-2011

☆ MONTPELIER
Green Mt. Club, 43 State St., has hiking guides & maps. Open weekdays year-round. 223-3463

Kent Museum, Maple Corner, was stagecoach tavern; general store, tours. Adm.; open July—Aug. & foliage weekends. 232-5660 or 828-2291

Morse Farm, County Rd., uses 25 miles of tubing to collect its sap; local crafts, samples. 223-2740

State Capitol, State St., is built of Barre granite; tours weekdays, daily in summer & foliage season. (Kids enjoy looking for fossil imprints in checkered VT marble floor.)

VT Museum, Pavilion Office Bldg., 109 State St., has things to touch, "What is it?" display; focus on Indians, industry & railroads. 828-2291

MORRISVILLE
Lamoille Valley RR, Stafford Ave., runs scenic trips through river valley. Fare; operates in summer. 888-4255

Noyes House Museum (c. 1820), Main St., displays various collections: costumes, dolls, military artifacts, toys; tours. Open July—Aug., foliage weekends. 888-5605

MT. SNOW
Mt. Snow Resort, off rte. 100, offers views of 4 states from chairlift. Adm.; runs summer—foliage season, ski season. 464-3333

NEWFANE
Common boasts more than 60 old buildings in variety of architectural styles.

Townshend SP, rte. 30 & Town Rd., offers hiking up Bald Mt. 365-7500

NEWPORT
Am. Maple Products, Union & Bluff Rds., runs tours of maple candy processing in restored railroad coach. Free; closed holidays. 334-6516

ORWELL
Mt. Independence, off rte. 73A, has Rev. War fortifications; trails through 400 acres of pasture & woods, views of Lake Champlain. Free; open June—mid-Oct. 828-3226

PITTSFORD
Federal Fish Hatchery, off rte. 7, raises landlocked salmon. Free; open daily. 483-6618

NE Maple Museum, rte. 7, has demonstrations, dioramas, tours. Preschoolers free; open daily mid-May—mid-Dec. 483-9414

PLYMOUTH
Coolidge SP, rte. 100A. 759-2354

Plymouth Notch Hist. Dist., off rte. 100A, includes Calvin Coolidge birthplace, General Store, Plymouth Cheese Factory, visitor center, Wilder House & Barn. Free for kids under 15; open daily June—mid-Oct. 838-3226

POULTNEY

Lake St. Catherine SP, rte. 30, has nature museum & trail, playground. 287-9158
Poultney Hist. Soc., E. Poultney, displays carriages, turn-of-century schoolhouse, old tools. Open Sun. p.m., July—Aug. 287-9834/-4042

PROCTOR

Marble Exhibit, Main St., displays quarrying & finishing work that put this area on the map; film. Adm.; open daily spring—fall. 459-3311
Wilson Castle, W. Proctor Rd., is 115-acre estate; aviary, carriage & gas house. Preschoolers free; open daily spring—fall. 773-3284

PUTNEY

River Valley Playhouse & Art Center, Landmark College, River Rd., has classes & performances year-round. 387-4355
Santa's Land, rte. 5 (Exit 4 or 5, I-91), is Christmas theme park; rides & petting zoo. Adm.; open May—Christmas. 387-5550

QUECHEE

Simon Pearce Glass, in The Mill, has demonstrations that fascinate kids.
Quechee Gorge SP, rte. 4 (Exit 1, I-89), is VT's answer to the Grand Canyon. 295-2990

ROCKINGHAM

Old Rockingham Meeting House, rte. 103, has interesting gravestones in burying ground & pigpen-style pews. Free to kids under 15; open daily in summer & 2 weeks in fall. 463-3964
VT Country Store, rte.

103, has old covered bridge, gristmill, soda fountain. Free; closed major holidays. 463-3855

RUTLAND

Norman Rockwell Museum, rte. 4E, displays large collection of artist's work. Adm.; open daily year-round. 773-6095
Rutland Lib., Court St., exhibits Tasha Tudor illustrations in Children's Room. Free; open Mon.—Sat. year-round. 773-1860
USDA Forest Service, 151 West St., has maps & information on Green Mt. Nat. Forest. 773-0300

ST. ALBANS

Burton Island SP is accessible only by passenger ferry from Kamp Kill Kare SP, Town Rd.; nature center, naturalist. 524-6353
Kamp Kill Kare SP, Town Rd., 3 1/2 miles off rte. 36, is another Lake Champlain park. 524-6021

ST. JOHNSBURY

Catamount Arts, 60 Eastern Ave., sponsors performances for kids. Adm.; open year-round. 748-2600
Fairbanks Museum & Planetarium, Main & Prospect Sts., exhibits over 2,500 stuffed birds & animals; planetarium shows (separate fee). Adm.; closed holidays. 748-2372
Maple Grove Museum, rte. 2, demonstrates process that turns sap into sugar; film, samples, tours. Kids under 12 free; open daily May—Oct. 748—5141
St. Johnsbury Athenaeum, in Lib. at 30 Main St., displays Am. paintings in US' oldest original gallery. Free; closed Sat. in summer. 748-8291

SHELBURNE

Am. Morgan Horse Museum, around corner from Shelburne Museum, 3 Bostwick Rd., plans to sponsor live demonstrations. 985-4944
Shelburne Farms, Harbor Rd., demonstrates cheese-making on 1,000-acre estate; tours. Adm.; open June—mid-Oct. 985-8686
Shelburne Museum & Heritage Park, rte. 7, is collection of 37 buildings from NE; sidewheeler *S.S. Ticonderoga*, carriage, coaches, decoys, dolls, farm & firefighting equipment, folk art, toys, collection of NE & Am. art. Adm.; open mid-May—mid-Oct. 985-3344

SPRINGFIELD

Eureka Schoolhouse, rte. 11, is 18th-century schoolhouse near covered bridge; exhibits, tours. Free; open daily June—mid-Oct. 828-3226
Springfield Art. & Hist. Soc., 9 Elm St., has costumes, dolls, exhibits of local history; classes for kids, tours. Open Tues.—Fri., May—Oct.
Stellafane Soc. Museum, Hartness House Inn, 30 Orchard St., has telescopes (one invented by Gov. James Hartness) for viewing; 5-room underground railway hiding place. Free; tours daily 11-9 (advance notice recommended). 885-2115

STOWE

Mt. Mansfield, accessible from Smugglers' Notch & Stowe, is VT's highest peak, 4,393'; State Forest covers 27,613 acres, Long Trail.
Smugglers' Notch SP, rte. 108, is a good base for

exploring Mt. Mansfield.
253-4014

Stowe Alpine Slide, rte.
108 at Spruce Peak, allows
riders to control their speed;
views. Adm.; open summer—foliage season. 253-
7311

Stowe Auto Rd., rte. 108,
is not recommended for
novice drivers. Fee, parking
at summit; open mid-June—mid-Oct. (weather permitting). 253-7311

Stowe Hist. Soc. Museum,
Main St., has restored 1-
room schoolhouse (by appt.);
clothes, photos of early
memorabilia in this resort,
old tools. Free; open Fri. &
Sat. 253-7305

Stowe Gondola, rte. 108,
offers spectacular views.
Adm.; open summer—foliage, ski season. 253-7311

STRAFFORD

**Justin Smith Morrill
Homestead**, rte. 132, is
Gothic Revival home of man
who wrote land-grant
college bill; 7 outbuildings.
Free; tours Wed.—Sun.,
June—mid-Oct. 828-3226

STRATTON MT.

Stratton Arts Festival,
Stratton Mt. Base Lodge,
demonstrates art, crafts,
mime, music, photography,
sculpture; performances.
Preschoolers free. 297-2200

Stratton Resort, rte. 30,
17 miles east of Manchester,
is year-round resort. 297-
2200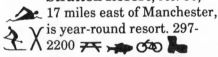

SWANTON

**Missisquoi Nat. Wildlife
Refuge**, rte. 78, has interpretive trail; bass, carp,
perch, pike, salmon, walleye. 868-4781

THETFORD HILL

Thetford Hill SP, rte.

113A to Academy Rd. (Exit
4, I-91), is free.

TUNBRIDGE

World's Fair features ox &
pony pulls, demolition
derby, arts & crafts demonstrations in log cabin. Adm.;
mid-Sept. 889-3458

VERGENNES

**Basin Harbor Maritime
Museum**, Basin Harbor, is
located in native-stone
schoolhouse; wooden boat
collection, exhibits of 10,000
years of lake history. Adm.;
open June—mid-Oct. 475-
2317

Bixby Mem. Free Lib., 258
Main St., displays large
collection of Indian artifacts,
works of VT artists, stamps.
Open year-round at various
times. 877-2211

Button Bay SP, off rte.
22A, Basin Harbor, has boat
rentals & dock on Lake
Champlain; naturalist, museum. 475-2377

WARREN

Canoe Vermont, c/o Mad
River Canoe, Waitsfield, has
guided expeditions, inn-to-inn canoe tours. 496-2409

Clearwater Sports, rte.
100, Waitsfield, offers canoe
trips, rents mountain bikes.
496-2708

Granville Gulf SP, rte.
100, has 6-mile scenic drive;
Moss Glen Falls, Mad River.

Sugarbush Resort, off rte.
100, offers upscale recreation year-round. 583-2381 or
800-53-SUGAR

WATERBURY

**Ben & Jerry's Ice Cream
Factory**, rte. 100 (Exit 10,
I-89), gives tours of 2.5
million-gallon business
every half-hour; movies on
summer eves. Kids under 12
free; open daily. 244-5641

Cold Hollow Cider Mill,
rte. 100 (Exit 10, I-89),
Waterbury Center, demonstrates cidermaking; free
samples. Free; open daily
year-round. 244-8771

Little River SP, rte. 2 to
Little River Rd., has trails
up Camel's Hump & Mt.
Mansfield; marked nature
walks, playground. 244-7103

Waterbury Center Beach,
off rte. 100. 244-7103

VT Country Cyclers,
Loomis Hill Rd., Waterbury
Center, rents bikes; has
tours, maps. 244-5215

W. DANVILLE

Goodrich's Sugarhouse,
off rte. 2, has guided tours,
trails. Free; open daily.

WESTON

Farrar-Mansur House, on
Common, was 18th-century
tavern; ballroom, clocks,
costumes, dolls, weaving &
spinning equipment. Donations; open June—mid-Oct.
824-6781

**Guild of Old Time Crafts
& Industries**, rte. 100, demonstrates traditional crafts
in 18th-century sawmill.
Free; open Wed.—Sun.,
summer—Columbus Day.
824-5288

VT Country Store, rte.
100, is turn-of-century
emporium. 824-3184

WILMINGTON

Molly Stark SP, rte. 9 (Exit
2, I-91), offers access to Mt.
Olga. 464-5460

WOODSTOCK

Billings Farm & Museum,
rte. 12 across Elm St.
Bridge, is modern dairy in
turn-of-century setting;
museum focuses on seasonal
farm tasks, like buttermaking, icecutting, sugaring.
Adm.; open daily spring—

fall. 457-2355

The Cyclery Plus, 36 rte. 4, W. Woodstock, has rentals, maps, tours. 457-3377

Woodstock Hist. Soc., 26 Elm St., displays costumes, dollhouses, farm equipment, toys in Dana family home; guided tours. Adm.; open daily, spring—fall. 457-1822

VT Inst. of Natural Science, Church Hill Rd. off rte. 4, is 80-acre preserve with self-guided trails, field trips & workshops; Raptor Center cares for injured birds, 26 flight habitats (no pets allowed). Adm.; open year-round. 457-2779

New Hampshire

Area code: 603

For information on state facilities, call 271-3254.

Appalachian Trail Conference, PO Box 807, Harpers Ferry, WV 25424, has detailed descriptions & maps in *Appalachian Trail Guide to New Hampshire & Vermont.* 304/535-6331

The Connecticut River Watershed Council, 312 First NH Bank Building, Lebanon, NH 03766, gives up-to-date information on river conditions for canoeists. 603/488-2792

ALLENTOWN

Bear Brook SP, off rte. 28, 5 miles northeast of Hooksett, is a large, forested area with a variety of activities; Audubon Nature Center offers free programs July & Aug. 485-3782

AMHERST

Ponemah Bog, Stearns Rd. off rte. 122, is a 100-acre botanical preserve with boardwalks & trails. 224-9909

BARTLETT

Attitash Alpine Slide, rte. 302, has summer water fun plus scenic views from chairlift. Adm.; open in summer (nearby ski area in winter). 374-2369

BETHLEHEM

Bretzfelder Park, Prospect St., has summer programs for kids; trails & trout ponds. Free; open year-round.

Rocks Estate, rte. 302 (Exit 40, I-93), offers hayrides on turn-of-century farm. 444-6228

BRETTON WOODS

Cog Railway, Cog RR Rd. off rte. 302 at Fabyan's Station, is Sylvester Marsh's unique way to climb Mt. Washington. 846-5404

Mt. Jefferson via Caps Ridge Trail, Jefferson Notch Rd. off Cog RR Rd., makes a marvelous hike for older kids.

BRISTOL

Wellington SP, off rte. 3A, is one of NH's best lake beaches.

CANTERBURY

Shaker Village (1792), 7 miles from Exit 18, I-93, offers exhibits & tours in one of NE's last Shaker communities; gourmet restaurant (reservations advised). Adm.; open spring—fall. 783-9511

CHARLESTOWN

Old Fort #4, rte. 11, 1 mile north of town, is a reproduction of the village which held off French & Indians; living history museum with costumed interpreters & hands-on activities. Adm.; open spring—fall. 826-5700

CHESTERFIELD

Chesterfield Gorge State Wayside, rte. 9, has footpaths cut in the gorge for those who want to see glacial action first-hand (hiking shoes advised). Free; open year-round.

Road's End Farm, Jackson Hill Rd., is working horse farm & riding camp with trails for day-trippers. 363-4703

Pisgah SP, rte. 63, 2 miles east of town, has 13,000 acres of wilderness; interpretive programs. Adm.; open year-round.

☆ CONCORD

Audubon House, 3 Silk Farm Rd. off Clinton St. (Exit 2, I-89), has games & touch table for kids; bird blind & resident owls. 224-9909

Chamber of Commerce, 244 Main St., has self-guided tours of historic area, beginning at Eagle Sq. Marketplace. 224-2508

Conservation Center, 54 Portsmouth St., offers self-guided tours of its new-age building & trails. Free; closed holidays & weekends. 224-9945

NH Hist. Soc. Museum, 30 Park St., has changing exhibits suitable for grade-school kids plus famous Concord coach. Donations; open daily year-round. 225-3381

Pierce Manse, 14 Penacook St., is the only home this President owned. Preschoolers free; open Mon.—Fri. in summer. 224-9620

Statehouse, 107 N. Main St., is made of NH granite & VT marble; visitor center, guided & self-guided tours. Free; open Mon.—Fri., closed holidays. 271-2154

Summer band concerts, Bicentennial Sq. or State House Plaza. Free; Tues. evenings in summer.

CONWAY

Kancamagus Hwy., rte. 112W, just south of town,

offers a scenic drive through the White Mt. Nat. Forest. **Madison Boulder**, rte. 113, Madison, is huge glacial erratic.

Saco Bound, rte. 302, Center Conway, offers guided canoe trips (some appropriate even for young kids), rentals & pick-up service. Open year-round. 447-2177

CORNISH has four covered bridges, including the longest such span in the US:

Augustus Saint-Gaudens Nat. Hist. Site, off rte. 12A, may be of interest to older, more artistic youngsters; sculpture demonstrations & exhibits plus summer concerts. Kids free; open spring—fall. 675-2175

N. Star Canoe & Bike Livery, rte. 12A on CT River, rents what you need to enjoy this part of the country; combines bike or canoe trips with overnights in country inns. 542-5802

CRAWFORD NOTCH
Arethusa Falls, off rte. 302, is a short, popular family hike.

Ripley Falls, off rte. 302, a 100-foot cascade, is a cool place to relax on the hottest day.

Willey House Site, rte. 302, offers parking for popular outdoor area; Appalachian Trail nearby.

DALTON
Forest Lake SP, off rte. 116, is an idyllic mountain beach; lifeguards & playground.

DERRY
Robert Frost Homestead, rte. 28, was home to the poet. Free for kids; open Wed.—Sun. in summer. 432-

3091
Taylor Up-and-Down Sawmill, jct. rte. 28 & 28 bypass, is a mechanized version of the two-man pit saw; operates in summer.

DIXVILLE NOTCH
The Balsams, rte. 26, is a winter/summer resort; only restaurant for miles. 675-5391

Dixville Notch SP, rte. 26, is the narrowest & northern-most White Mt. pass; gorge & waterfalls.

DOVER
Woodman Institute, 182-192 Central Ave., has 3 hist. buildings, including old garrison & abolitionist's home. Donation; closed Mon. & holidays. 742-1038

DUBLIN
The Friendly Farm, rte. 101, has livestock & their young for feeding & petting; observation beehive. Adm.; open spring—fall. 563-8444

EPPING
Rum Brook Farm, rte. 87E off rte. 125, has Morgan horse barn open Sun. Adm.; open spring—fall. 679-5982/ 436-4652

FITZWILLIAM
Rhododendron SP, off rte. 12, has plants blooming in July; trails.

FRANCONIA
Cannon Mt., Fr. Notch Pkwy., has aerial tramway with spectacular views & trails to alpine flowers. Adm.; open summer, fall, ski season. Ski Museum, under 12 free with adult; open spring—fall, ski season. 823-5563 (tramway); 823-7177 (museum).

Franconia Notch SP, I-93

to Fr. Notch Pkwy., has some of NH's most beautiful mountain scenery; The Basin, Echo Lake, the Flume (adm. to visitor center), Old Man of the Mountain; 823-5563. Connections to Mt. Lafayette, Appalachian Trail & App. Mt. Club huts (Lonesome Lake camp is an excellent family shelter; reservations: 466-2727).

The Frost Place, rte. 116 to signs (Exit 38, I-93), is another farmhouse where the poet lived & worked; readings. Preschoolers free; open Wed.—Mon., July & Aug.; weekends, May & Sept. 823-5510

FRANKLIN
Daniel Webster Birth-place, off rte. 127, is a humble two-room frame home; summer theater (adm.). Kids under 18 free; open Wed.—Sun. in summer. 934-4873

Webster Lake, rte. 11, offers scuba diving; fee.

GILFORD
Alpine Ridge, rte. 11A, has 9 ways to slide. Adm.; open daily in summer. 293-4304

Ellacoya State Beach, rte. 11, is 600' beach with mountain views.

Gunstock Recreation Area, rte. 11A, is a county-owned year-round resort; paddleboats, playground, horseback riding.

GILSUM
Old stone-arch bridge at Ashuelot Gorge, off rte. 10, is an unusual structure in state known for its covered bridges.

Gilsum Public Library, rte. 10, sells (at prices kids can afford) maps of more than 50 old mines for exploring & rock collecting; annual rock festival (of the mineral, rather than heavy-metal variety). 357-0320

GLEN

Grand Manor Antique & Classic Car Museum, rte. 16, has Bonnie & Clyde's Ford plus old-time radio shows; summer concerts. Adm.; open daily in summer, weekends only spring & fall. 356-9366

Heritage NH, rte. 16, recreates state history "involv-arounding" sights, sounds, smells. Adm.; open daily summer—fall. 383-9776

Story Land, rte. 16, is a low-key fairy tale park with animals & rides, ideal for younger kids. Adm.; open summer & fall. 383-4293

GORHAM

Moose Brook SP, off rte. 2, 2 miles west of town, is another base for hiking the Presidentials or stream-fishing.

Working Vacations, PO Box 298C, Gorham, 03851, gives kids & families opportunities for public-service outdoor vacations; Adopt-A-Trail, Adopt-A-Shelter, other volunteer programs. 466-2721

GRAFTON

Ruggles Mine (1803), rte. 4 to signs & orange arrows, has a mine pit & tunnels open for rock hounds; small shop sells & rents picks. Adm.; open summer & fall. 448-6911 or 763-2495

GREENFIELD

Greenfield SP, rte. 136, 1 mile west of town, separates campers from day-trippers on its 400 acres along Otter Lake.

GROTON

Sculptured Rocks, rtes. 3A & 118, 2 miles west of town, has glacially-formed potholes.

HAMPTON

Casino Cascade Waterslide, D St. Adm.; open daily in summer. 926-4541

Hampton Beach SP, rte. 1A, is very popular (lifeguards, supervised playground); Seashell has nightly entertainment. Adm. 800/438-2826

Hampton Playhouse, 357 Winnacunnet Rd., offers summer stock with shows for kids. Adm. 926-3073

Olde Port Trolley Co., Hampton Beach, has narrated rides along the beach. Adm.; runs daily in summer. 692-5111

Smith & Gilmore Fishing Pier, Ocean Blvd., runs deep-sea fishing, whale-watching trips. 926-3503

HANCOCK

Covered bridge over Contoocook River.

DePierrefeu-Willard Pond Sanctuary & Nature Center, rte. 123, 3 miles north of village, offers over 800 acres to explore. 224-9909

Harris Center For Conservation Ed., King's Hwy., has star watches; nature trails open daily. Free. 525-4073

HANOVER

Hiking information is available from Dartmouth Outing Club, Dartmouth College 03755; 646-2440.

Hood Museum, Dartmouth Green, has changing exhibits for older elem. kids; art & anthropology collections. Free; open when college is in session, closed Mon. 646-

2808/-2900

Montshire Museum of Science, 45 Lyme Rd., rte. 10, makes natural science appealing to youngsters; family programs & field trips. (Moving across the river in the fall, 1989.) Adm.; closed major holidays. 643-5672

HEBRON

Paradise Point Nature Center, N. Shore Rd. (Exit 26, I-93 to rte. 3A), has self-guided trails through 43 acres of woods on Newfound Lake; kids' programs, naturalist on staff. Adm.; open daily in summer. 744-3516

HILLSBORO

Fox State Forest, Center Rd., has a forestry museum; information on local animals & plants plus ecology walks.

Hot Air Ballooning, Sawmill Rd. 478-5666

Franklin Pierce Homestead (1804), rtes. 9 & 31, was the President's boyhood home. Free to kids; open in summer. 478-3165

HOLDERNESS

Golden Pond Cruise, The Manor, rte. 3 & Shepard Hill Rd., offers 2-hr. cruises on the lake "Golden Pond" made famous; narration on loons. Fee; runs late spring—fall. 968-3348

Science Center of NH, rtes. 3 & 113, has native animals in natural habitats plus games & activities for all ages. Adm.; open daily in summer, weekends in spring & fall. 968-7194

Squam Lakeside Farm, rte. 113, rents boats for use on Little Squam Lake; 968-7227. Public beach nearby (rtes. 113 & 175).

HOPKINTON
Chase Wildlife Sanctuary, Jewett Rd. (Exit 4, I-89), managed by NH Audubon Soc., has trails through marsh to beaver dam. 224-9909

JAFFREY
Monadnock Ecocenter, off rte. 124, is popular with hikers for views of NE states; audio-visuals & exhibits. Free; open summer & fall. 532-8035
Monadnock Music concerts (17 towns); 924-7610.
Old Burying Ground, off rte. 124 Jaffrey Center, is a good place to make gravestone rubbings (contact selectmen for permission); Willa Cather & Amos Fortune buried here, old horse barns & meetinghouse with Revere bell.
Silver Ranch & Airpark, rte. 124, offers carriage rides, hayrides, scenic plane trips (reservations advised). Fee; open daily. 532-7363 (stable); 532-8870 (plane).

JEFFERSON
Santa's Village & Gingerbread Forest, rte. 2, has animals & woods in addition to theme park. Adm.; open summer & fall. 586-4445
Six Gun City, rte. 2, has rides & waterslide. Adm.; open summer & fall. 586-4592

KEENE
Horatio Colony Wildlife Sanctuary, Daniels Hill Rd., 1 mile west of rtes. 10, 12 & 101, has trails through 450 acres. Free; open daily.

KINSMAN NOTCH
Lost River, rte. 112 west of Lincoln, offers caverns & geological wonders; nature garden includes ferns & mosses. Adm.; open summer & fall. 745-8031

LANCASTER
Weeks SP, off rte. 3, was mountaintop home of man who helped found nat. forest system; mansion with exhibits. Kids free; open summer & fall. 788-4004

LINCOLN
Fantasy Farm & Whale's Tale Water Park, rte. 3, has petting zoo plus rides. Adm.; open summer. 745-8810
Hobo RR, rte. 3 (Exit 33, I-93), offers kid-length train rides along Pemigewasset River; ferris wheel, evening concerts. Preschoolers free; open summer & fall. 745-2135
Kancamagus Hwy., rte. 112 between Conway & Lincoln, is a wonderful escape into White Mt. Nat. Forest; Boulder Loop Trail, Champney Falls, Lower Falls, Rail 'n River Nature Trail, Sabbaday Falls are fun for families. Information at Ranger Station; 745-8720.
Loon Mt. Gondola Skyride, Kancamagus Hwy., gives wonderful White Mt. views; nature trail & tower. Adm.; open summer & ski season. 745-8111

MANCHESTER
Currier Gallery, 192 Orange St. (Exit 4, I-293), displays art plus NH crafts; concerts. Free; closed Mon. & holidays. 669-6144
Manchester Hist. Assoc. Museum, 129 Amherst St. (Exit 4, I-93), has firefighting equipment, Indian artifacts & belongings of Gen. Stark. Free; closed Sun., Mon. & holidays. 622-7531
NH Performing Arts Center, 80 Hanover St. (Exit 4, I-293), hosts family entertainment. Adm.; open year-round. 668-5588
Scouting Museum, Camp Carpenter, Bodwell Rd. Free; open daily in summer. 669-8919

MASON
Pickity Place, Nutting Hill Rd. off rte. 31, is an herb farm where the Caldecott-winning illustrator of *Little Red Riding Hood* lived; exhibits & lunch (reservations & charge). Free; open year-round. 878-1151

MILTON
NH Farm Museum, rte. 16, displays old tools & crafts in state's best-preserved farm buildings; tours & special events. Adm.; open Fri.—Sun., summer & fall. 652-7840

MOULTONBOROUGH
Castle in the Clouds, rte. 171, is inventor's dream home; pony rides, walking trails, views. Adm.; open summer & fall. 476-2352
Old Country Store & Museum, rtes. 25 & 109. Free; open daily year-round. 476-5750

MT. SUNAPEE
Mt. Sunapee SP, rte. 103B (Exit 12A, I-89), has chairlift for views (fee) & beach. Kids under 12 free; open spring—fall. 763-2356
M/V Kearsarge, Steamboat Landing, offers lake cruises in Victorian splendor. Fare; runs in summer. 763-5477
M/V Mt. Sunapee II, Sunapee Harbor, offers 90-min. lake cruises. Fare; runs spring—fall. 763-4030
Osborne's Marine, rte. 11, Sunapee Harbor, (Exit 12A, I-89), rents boats & water

skiing equipment. Fees; open spring—fall. 763-2611

MT. WASHINGTON
Auto Rd. & Stages, rte. 16 at Glen House, provide breath-taking views up the northeast's highest peak; museum in Summit Bldg. (Hiking is recommended only for families with older kids & those prepared for adverse weather conditions in any season — it can snow here in summer! Trails lead to App. Mt. Club huts & Alpine Gardens). Fee; open summer & fall, weather permitting. 466-3988

NEW CASTLE
Ft. Constitution, rte. 1B at Coast Guard Station, was originally a British fort that NH patriots raided for arms to fight Revolution.
Great Island Common, rte. 1B, is 30 acres of waterfront in one of NH's most charming seacoast villages.

NORTH CONWAY
Conway Scenic RR, rtes. 16 & 302, offers hour-long scenic train rides. Fare; open spring—fall. 356-5251
Echo Lake SP, West Side Rd., is a lovely mountain lake reflecting ledges popular with climbers & hikers.
Fun Factory, rte. 16, has a waterslide where Dad & kids can cool off while Mom shops at nearby outlet malls. Fee; open summer. 356-6541
Mt. Cranmore Skimobile, rte. 16 to Kearsarge St. to signs, offers rides up the mountain, winter or summer; hiking trails & views. 356-5543

NOTTINGHAM
Pawtuckaway SP, Deer-

field Rd. off rte. 156, is a pleasant place to hike — even on a rainy day!

PETERBOROUGH
Miller SP, off rte. 101, 3 miles west of town, has an auto road up Pack Monadnock & views.
Peterborough Hist. Soc., Grove St. near Main, displays dolls & artifacts; country store, colonial kitchen, millworker's home. Free; open July—Oct. 924-3235

PINKHAM NOTCH
Joe Dodge Center, Pinkham Notch Camp, rte. 16, is App. Mt. Club's hiking headquarters; comfortable base camp, workshops. 466-2727
Wildcat Mt. Gondola, rte. 16, offers incredible views of Mt. Washington Valley; trails nearby. Fare; open summer, fall & winter.

PITTSBURG
Lake Francis SP, River Rd. off rte. 3, is a huge man-made lake in prime salmon & trout territory.

PITTSFIELD
White's Farm, S. Pittsfield Rd., has miniature horses & other mini animals to pet. Adm.; open daily except in rain, spring—fall. 435-8258

PLYMOUTH
Mary Baker Eddy Hist. House, Stinson Lake Rd., off rte. 25, Rumney. Adm.; open spring—fall, closed Mon. & holidays. 786-9943
Polar Caves, rte. 25, 5 miles west of town, make a cool adventure in the hottest weather. Adm.; open spring—fall. 536-1888
Quincy Bog, off rtes. 25/3A Rumney, is a 40-acre peat

bog with a resident botanist Tues.—Thurs.; tours. Free; nature center open in summer, bog open year-round. 786-9812
NH Music Festival, Plymouth State College (Exit 25, I-93), hosts summer performances. 536-5000, Ext. 2589

PORTSMOUTH
The Children's Museum of Portsmouth, Marcy St. near Prescott Park, offers 12 different hands-on exhibits, including lobster boat & the Yellow Submarine, a multi-level play area. Adm.; open year-round. 436-3853
Isles of Shoals Steamship Co./Oceanic Expeditions, Barker Wharf, 315 Market St. (Exit 7, I-95), runs narrated cruises out to the islands (free tour) & inland to Great Bay; whale watching. Fare; runs spring—fall. 431-5500
Portsmouth Trail is a walking tour of historic district; includes many fine old homes, like that of John Paul Jones. Adm.; open summer & fall. 436-1118
Prescott Park, 105 Marcy St. near drawbridge, offers spectacular flower gardens, free Broadway musicals on summer evenings & kids' art classes. Sheafe Warehouse Museum exhibits Piscataqua River boats. Free. 431-8748
Strawberry Banke, Marcy St., next to Prescott Park, is 10-acre living history community with craft demonstrations, old homes, gardens. Adm.; open daily May—Oct. 433-1100
Urban Forestry Center, 45 Elwyn Rd. at rte. 1 (Exit 5, I-95), offers tree ID trail, garden for the senses, historic house. Adm.; open daily year-round. 431-6774

USS Albacore - **Port of Portsmouth Maritime Park**, 500 Market St. Ext. (Exit 7, I-95), was one of our fastest & quietest submarines; tours & film. Adm.; open daily. 436-1331

Water Country, rte. 1 (Exit 5, I-95), has tubes, slides, wave pool plus kiddie area. Adm.; open daily in summer. 436-3556

Wentworth-Coolidge Mansion, Little Harbor Rd. off Sagamore Ave., was home to Royal Gov. who granted land to settlers in NH & VT; views. Kids free; open summer only, closed Mon. & Tues. 436-6607

RYE

Jenness State Beach, rte. 1A, is a half-mile stretch of white sand; small metered parking area, changing area, lifeguards. Adm.; open in summer.

NH Seacoast Cruises, Ocean Blvd. (rte. 1A) in Rye Harbor, offers lobstering trips & whale watching; cruises to the Isles of Shoals. Fare; runs daily in summer. 964-5545/382-6743

Odiorne Point SP, rte. 1A, was the first settlement in NH; 137 acres with drowned forest & Audubon nature center. Touch tank, films & family programs. Kids under 13 free; open in summer. 436-7406

Rye Harbor SP, rte. 1A, is a rocky point between ocean & harbor. Adm. in summer.

SALEM

America's Stonehenge, Haverhill Rd., 1 mile off rte. 111 (Exit 3, I-93), N. Salem, has early stone structures with astronomical markers. Adm.; open spring—fall. 893-8300

Canobie Lake Park, Exit 2, I-93, offers a variety of games & rides. Adm.; open spring & summer. 893-3506

SANDWICH has one of NH's best old-fashioned fairs every October:

Sandwich Hist. Soc. Museum, rte. 113, has Indian dugout canoe, replicas of old country store & post office. Free; open in summer. 284-6269

Sandwich Notch Rd. is a one-lane, dirt road over the mountain, linking rte. 49 in Waterville with Center Sandwich; not maintained in winter.

TAMWORTH

White Lake SP, rte. 16, is a popular camping area with sandy beach & trout fishing.

WARNER

Rollins SP, off rte. 103, has a road up Mr. Kearsarge with scenic views. Kids under 12 free; open summer & fall. 456-3808

WATERVILLE VALLEY

is a popular year-round resort area. 236-8311

Festival of the Arts, rte. 49 (Exit 28, I-93), offers summer concerts. Adm.; summer only. 236-8371

WEARE

Clough SP, off rte. 114, has a 115-acre river pool with large beach.

WEIRS BEACH

Funspot, rte. 3, is video-game heaven; rides for younger kids. Fees; open year-round, 24 hours daily in summer. 366-4377

Surf Coaster, rte. 3, is NH's first wave pool; Kiddie Play Park, miniature golf, videogames. Adm.; open daily in summer. 366-4991

Weirs Beach Water Slide, rte. 3, is a maze of tubing overlooking lake; various skill levels. Adm.; open daily in summer. 366-5161

Winnipesaukee Flagship Co. has boat trips of various lengths to Alton Bay, Center Harbor & Wolfeboro. Fare; runs in summer. 366-5531/-4837

Winnipesaukee RR, station above dock, connects NH's biggest lake with quieter spots; scenic views. Fare; runs summer & fall. 528-2330

WILMOT

Winslow SP, rte. 11, is a wonderful place to watch the sunset.

WILTON

Andy's Summer Playhouse, Wilton Center, has productions for kids. Adm. 654-2613

Frye's Measure Mill, rte. 31, dates back to 1750; older kids will enjoy demonstrations of early crafts & waterpower. Kids under 12 free; open May—Dec., closed Sun. & Mon. 654-6581

WOLFEBORO

Kingswood Summer Theatre for Children, in regional high school, offers workshops & plays. 569-3593

Libby Museum, rte. 109, exhibits Indian artifacts & tools; natural history displays. Adm.; open summer & fall.

Gov. John Wentworth Hist. Site, rte. 109, becomes archeological dig in summer.

Wolfeboro Friends of Music offers summer programs throughout town. Adm. 569-3714/-2428

MAINE

Area code: 207
For information on state facilities, call 289-2423.

Allagash Wilderness Waterway SP is a 92-mile corridor for outdoor adventure along lakes & river. 289-3821 (in summer); 723-8518 (rest of year).

Arnold Trail runs 194 miles from Fort Popham on Kennebec River to Coburn Gore on Canadian border, following historic route of Benedict Arnold (old forts en route); interpretive panels at 9 sites.

☆AUGUSTA

Augusta SP, between statehouse & river, has native & exotic trees, shrubs & ferns.

ME State Museum, State House at State & Capitol Sts., has exhibits of state's natural history, industry, lumbering, 1,000 products made in Maine. Free; closed holidays. 289-2301

BANGOR

Chamber of Commerce, 519 Main St., has self-guided walking tour. 947-0307

Mt. Katahdin Cruises, Bangor Public Landing, runs narrated tours of Penobscot River. Adm.; open Fri.—Sun., spring & fall. 945-0072

Paul Bunyan statue, Main St., points up the importance of lumbering in this part of ME.

BAR HARBOR/ MT. DESERT ISLAND was summer home of millionaires Morgan & Rockerfeller:

Abbe Museum of Stone Age Antiquities, near town, displays relics from stone age to Indians. Kids free; open daily mid-May to mid-Oct.

Acadia Nat. Park combines unusual mountain & ocean scenery on 40 sq. miles of Mt. Desert Island. Trails, carriage roads, scenic drives; extensive interpretive programs, many geared for children. Adm.; park open year-round, visitor center open daily in summer & fall. 288-3338

Echo Lake, rte. 102, south of Somesville, is popular beach; lifeguards. Free; open summer. 288-3338

Frenchman's Bay Boating Co., Bar Harbor municipal pier, runs 2-hr. cruises with park naturalist on board. Fare; open summer & fall. 288-5741

Mt. Desert Oceanarium, Clark Pt. Rd., exhibits live specimens of coastal marine life. Lobster room, touch tank. Adm.; open Mon.—Sat., mid-May to mid-Oct. 244-7330

Natural History Museum, rte. 3, at College of the Atlantic, 1.5 miles north of town, displays mounted maritime wildlife; backbone of model whale skeleton can be disassembled, Discovery Corner. Fee; open daily in summer. 288-5015

Wendell Gilley Museum, Main St. & Herrick Rd., exhibits 200 bird models by master carver. Audiovisual presentation, woodcarving demonstrations. Adm.; open Tues.—Sun., April—Dec. Closed holidays. 244-7555

BATH

ME Maritime Museum, 263 Washington St., recreates local wooden boat industry on 10 acres; restored schooner can be boarded. Lobstering exhibit; boat ride on Kennebec River in summer (fee). Sewall House has collection of maritime art & artifacts; children's room. Adm.; open daily year-round. 443-1316

BLUE HILL is a popular summer resort & crafts center:

Kneisel Hall Summer Music Center presents recitals by young performers during summer.

BOOTHBAY HARBOR has numerous cruise & fishing boats for hire:

Boothbay Railway Village, rte. 27, 3.5 miles north of town, exhibits railroad memorabilia & antique cars; 24 restored buildings, train rides. Fee; open daily in summer. 633-4727

Maine Aquarium, 2 miles southeast on McKown's Point, displays many varieties of fish. Free; open daily in summer. 289-2291 or 633-5572

BRISTOL

Colonial Pemaquid, off rte. 130, is archeological excavation of 17th & 18th century structures; museum displays prehistoric to colonial period artifacts. Adjacent is Fort William Henry, a replica of 1692 fortification for defense against Indians. Adm.; open daily in summer. 677-2423

Lighthouse Park, rte. 130, has museum. Kids under 13 free; open daily in summer. 677-2494

BRUNSWICK
Chamber of Commerce, 59 Pleasant St., offers historic walking tour for small fee. 725-8797
Bowdoin College, Bath & College Sts., gives tours of the school that Hawthorne, Longfellow, Peary & Pierce attended. 725-3000
Brunswick Fishway, off rte. 201 at Androscoggin River Dam, has fish ladder, viewing area & aquarium. Free; open daily in summer, Mon.—Fri. rest of year.
Museum of Art, Walker Art Building, Bowdoin campus, exhibits Winslow Homer collection. Free; closed Mon. & major holidays. 725-3275
Peary-MacMillan Arctic Museum, Hubbard Hall, Bowdoin campus, has displays from Arctic explorations. Free; closed Mon. & holidays. 725-3416

CALAIS, on Canadian border, is an international city:
 Moosehorn Nat. Wildlife Refuge, 3 miles southwest on Charlotte Rd., or second parcel 2 miles southeast of Dennysville on Cobscook Bay, is migratory bird refuge containing nature & hiking trails on 22,666 acres. Free; open daily. 454-3521

CAMDEN
Amphitheatre & Marine Park, Atlantic Ave., has concerts & art show.
Camden Hills SP, rte. 1, 2 miles north of town, offers camping & 30 miles of trails. Mt. Battie, which can

be hiked or driven, offers superb harbor views. Adm.; open daily May—Oct. 236-3109
Chamber of Commerce, foot of Commerce St., has self-guided walking tour.

CAPE ELIZABETH is an attractive suburb of Portland:
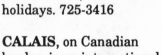 **Crescent Beach SP**, rte. 77, 8 miles south of Portland, offers 2 beaches & occasional views of harbor seals. Adm.; open daily in summer. 767-3625
Two Lights SP, 1/2 mile north of Crescent Beach, has 2 lighthouses, dramatic cliffs, crashing surf & woodland trails. Adm.; open mid-April—Nov. 799-5871

CARIBOU
Nylander Museum, 393 Main St., displays extensive collection of a self-taught naturalist. Free; open Wed.—Sun. in summer, weekends rest of year; closed Jan.—Feb. 493-4474

CASTINE has several old forts:
The State of Maine, ME Maritime Academy dock, was luxury passenger ship converted into troop transport during Korean War. Guided tours daily when in port, usually July—April. Free. 326-4311
Perkins House, next to Wilson Museum, is pre-Rev. War home; blacksmith shop & old hearses on grounds. Free (except guided tour of house); open Wed. & Sun. in summer. 326-8753
Wilson Museum, Perkins St., exhibits prehistoric material from Europe, Africa & the Americas; local Indian artifacts, rocks, minerals, colonial items.

Free; open in summer, closed Mon. 326-8753

DENNYSVILLE
Cobscook Bay SP, rte. 1, 4 miles south of town, has 24-foot tidal currents, campsites at water's edge. Adm.; open mid-May—Oct. 726-4412

DOVER-FOXCROFT
Peaks-Kenny SP, end of rte. 153, offers many activities & interpretive programs on shores of mountain lake. Adm.; open mid-May—Sept. 564-2003

EAST ORLAND
Craig Brook Nat. Fish Hatchery, off rte. 1, is oldest salmon hatchery in US. Visitor center, display pools, beach, trails. Free; open daily in summer. 469-2803

EAST WINTHROP
Winthrop Gem & Mineral Shop, rtes. 202/11/100, exhibits minerals & Indian artifacts & offers gold-panning field trip information. Free; open April—Dec., closed Sun. 395-4488

EDGECOMB
Fort Edgecomb, off rte. 1, is 1808 blockhouse with fortifications on Sheepscot River; harbor seals often sighted. Free; open daily in summer. 882-7777

ELLSWORTH
The Black House (c. 1820), W. Main St., has carriage house with carriages & sleighs. Adm.; open in summer, closed Sun. 667-8671
Stanwood Homestead (1850) Museum & Birdsacre Sanctuary, rte. 3, was home to pioneering ornithologist; 100-acre

wildlife sanctuary; rehabilitation facilities house many species, including hawks & owls. Museum (adm.) open daily in summer; sanctuary (donation) open year-round. 667-8460

FALMOUTH
ME Audubon Society, Gilsland Farm, off rte. 1, offers extensive family programs, nature trails on 70 acres. Free; open daily year-round. 781-2330

FARMINGTON
Little Red Schoolhouse Museum, rtes. 2 & 4, 2 miles west of town, is restored 1-room schoolhouse. Donations; open daily in summer. 778-4172

THE FORKS
Northern Outdoors offers white water rafting trips on Dead, Kennebec & Penobscot Rivers. Fee; open April—Oct. 664-4466
Rolling Thunder has similar excursions May—Oct. 663-4441

FORT KENT
Fort Kent State Hist. Site, off Main St., is hand-hewn blockhouse built in 1839 during bloodless Aroostook Border War; museum of lumbering & Indian artifacts. Free; open daily in summer. 764-2041

FREEPORT
Bradbury Mt. SP, Pownal Center (Exit 20, I-95), has panoramic views of Casco Bay & countryside. Adm.; open spring—fall. 688-4712
Desert of ME, 2 miles west of Freeport on Desert Rd. (Exit 19, I-95), is 100 acres of unique inland sand dunes; self-guided tours, nature trails, narrated

coach tours, farm museum & Sand Museum. Adm.; open daily end of May to mid-Oct. 865-6962
Mast Landing Audubon Sanctuary, east of rte. 1, is 150 acres of woods, fields & marshland with extensive trail network. 781-2330
Wolfe's Neck Woods SP, 1 mile beyond Mast Landing, has 200 acres of woodland trails on rocky peninsula; some trails with balancing beams for kids, active interpretation program. Adm.; open daily in summer, guided walks available year-round. 865-4465

GRAY
State Game Farm Visitor Center, off rte. 26, has self-guided trails through game farm; trout pools. Free; open April—Nov. 657-4977

GREENVILLE
Eastern River Expeditions offers overnight white water rafting trips for all levels of ability. 695-2411 or 800/634-RAFT (outside ME)
Katahdin, at center of town, is restored 1914 steamship which makes sightseeing trips on Moosehead Lake. Fee; departs daily in summer. 695-2716
Moosehead Marine Museum displays memorabilia pertaining to lake ships. Free; open daily in summer. 695-2716

HIRAM
Hiram Falls Nature Area, off rte. 113, has self-guided trail. Free; open daily.

KENNEBUNK
Brick Store Museum, 117 Main St., displays seafaring & shipbuilding memorabilia.

Adm.; open Tues.—Sat. year-round; closed holidays. 985-4802
Wedding Cake House, rte. 35/9A, is ornate Victorian confection among elegant ship captain's houses (privately-owned but picture-taking allowed).

KENNEBUNKPORT is
President Bush's summer home:
Parson's Way, at the end of Ocean Ave., is scenic coastal drive with the President's summer cottage on a point — Secret Service personnel at gate.
Seashore Trolley Museum, off rte. 1 on Log Cabin Rd., has large collection of antique trolley cars. Rides, museum, guided tours. Adm.; open daily in summer, weekends June & Sept. 967-2712

KITTERY
Fort McClary State Hist. Site, rte. 103, is 1846 blockhouse overlooking Piscataqua River. Adm. for building, grounds free. Open daily in summer, weekends only spring & fall.
Kittery Hist. & Naval Museum, rtes. 1 & 236, exhibits shipbuilding items, with emphasis on Portsmouth (NH) Naval Shipyard. Adm.; open Mon.—Sat. in summer & fall, Sats. only rest of year. 439-3080

LIBERTY
Lake St. George SP, rte. 3, has beach with lifeguards, boat launch. Adm.; open mid-May—Sept. 589-4255

LIVERMORE
Norlands Living History Center, off rte. 108 on Norlands Rd., offers guided tours on 445-acre working

farm, with 19th-century mansion, schoolhouse, farmer's cottage, church & barn. Time Machine journeys back into 1800's (year-round by appt.). Adm.; open Wed.—Sun., July—Aug. 897-2236/-6608

LUBEC
Campobello Island, across Narrows in Canada, has 3,000-acre park; 34-room cottage where Franklin D. Roosevelt summered. Free; open summer & fall. 752-2997

Quoddy Head SP & West Quoddy Lighthouse, 4 miles off rte. 189, consists of 481 acres of rocky cliffs 80' above Atlantic at easternmost point in US; trails include boardwalk leading into peat bog. Free; park open summer & fall, lighthouse grounds open daily year-round. 764-2041

MACHIASPORT
Gates House (c. 1807), off rte. 92, exhibits local artifacts & models of ships engaged in first naval battle of Am. Rev. War. Donations; open in summer, Mon.—Fri. 255-8461

Fort O'Brien, near Gates House, was destroyed by British in 1814; earthworks overlooking Machias Bay.

Monhegan Island is a cluster of spruces & dramatic cliffs; many artists' studios open to public, well-marked hiking trails, sanctuary, museum on Lighthouse Hill. Accessible by ferry:

Balmy Days Island Cruises leaves from Boothbay Harbor, fee. 633-2284

Hardy Boat Cruises, Shaw's Lobster Wharf, departs from New Harbor;

puffin trips to Easter Egg Rock, seal watches, lobster-haul demonstrations. Fee; leaves daily in summer. 677-2026

Monhegan-Thomaston Boat Line leaves from Port Clyde; fee. 372-8848

MONMOUTH
Monmouth Museum, center of town, consists of 8 buildings displaying ME rural life in 19th century. Adm. (buy tickets at stencil shop); open Tues.—Sun. in summer. 933-4444

NAPLES
Sebago Lake SP, between Naples & S. Casco off rte. 302, offers extensive sand beaches (lifeguards), camping, ranger-conducted programs & hikes; popular fishing spot. Fee; open daily May—mid-Oct. 693-6231

Songo River Queen II is sternwheel river boat that cruises from Long Lake down Songo River & through Songo Lock to Sebago Lake. Fee; daily trips in summer, weekends June & Sept. 693-6861

NEWRY
Grafton Notch SP, rte. 26 north of Bethel, offers many hiking trails in spectacular mountain scenery. Interpretive panels detail natural history. Free; open mid-May—mid-Oct. 824-2912

NEWFIELD
Willowbrook at Newfield is restored 33-building village. Adm.; open daily mid-May—Sept. 793-2784

OGUNQUIT
Finestkind Scenic Cruises, Perkins Cove, offers narrated lobstering trips, cruises. Fee; operates

daily June—mid-Oct. 646-5227

Marginal Way, Perkins Cove, is spectacular mile-long paved cliff walk. Free; open daily year-round.

OLD ORCHARD BEACH
The Ball Park, off rte. 5, is home to ME Phillies, Philadelphia farm team; games from mid-April to Sept. Adm. 934-4561

Palace Playland, rte. 9, has antique carousel, rides, waterslide, arcade. Adm.; open daily in summer. 934-2001

PATTEN
Lumberman's Museum, rte. 159, has 2,500 logging exhibits in 9 buildings, including full-scale replica of 1820's lumber camp. Adm.; open Tues.—Sun. in summer. 528-2650/-2547

PHILLIPS
Sandy River RR Park, rte. 142, offers mile-long rides on restored narrow gauge railroad. Adm.; open May—Nov., 1st & 3rd Sun. 353-8382

POPHAM
Fort Popham, rte. 209, is semi-circular granite fort used in Civil War. Free; open in summer. 389-1335

Popham Beach SP, 2 miles north of Ft. Popham, is long stretch of sand. 389-1335

PORTLAND
Casco Bay Lines, Ferry Terminal, Franklin & Commercial Sts., runs 24 sightseeing cruises while carrying mail & commuters. Fee; departures daily. 774-7871

Children's Museum of ME, 746 Stevens Ave., has participatory displays for kids up to 10 years, including firehouse room, doctor's office, grocery store, physical fitness room. Adm.; open daily year-round. 797-KITE

Children's Resource Center, 741 Stevens Ave., sells recycled items at affordable prices for kids' creative projects. Free; open daily year-round. 797-0525

♪ **Kinderkonzerts** is a concert series performed by Portland Symphony Orchestra to introduce kids to musical instruments. Open Oct.—May; reservations advised. 773-8191

Longfellow Cruise Line, Commercial St. at Long Wharf, has harbor sightseeing excursions, including lobster fisheries & island history cruise, lighthouse & shipwreck cruise, & naturalist cruise. Fee; leaves daily April—Nov. 774-3578

Portland Observatory, 138 Congress St., offers harbor views from 82-foot octagonal wooden signal tower. Adm.; open Wed.—Sun. in summer. 774-5561

Southworth Planetarium, Science Building, Univ. of Southern ME, off rtes. 25 & 100, has changing astronomical shows. Adm.; open mid-Sept.—June, Sun., Wed., Fri. eves. 780-4249

PRESQUE ISLE

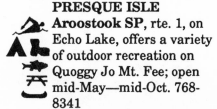 **Aroostook SP**, rte. 1, on Echo Lake, offers a variety of outdoor recreation on Quoggy Jo Mt. Fee; open mid-May—mid-Oct. 768-8341

PROSPECT

Fort Knox Hist. Site, rte. 174, is well-preserved granite fortification; interpretive program. Fee; open May—Nov. 469-7719

RANGELEY

 Rangeley Lake SP, between rtes. 4 & 17, offers mountain lake scenery. Fee; open mid-May—Sept. 864-3858

RICHMOND

Steve Powell Wildlife Mgmt. Area (Swan Island), accessible by ferry from Richmond, has camping & self-guided nature trails. Fee for ferry; open daily May—Aug. 737-8149

ROCKLAND

Farnsworth Art Museum, 19 Elm St., is large collection of ME artists, including Andrew Wyeth; Greek Revival home next door (fee). Students free; open daily in summer, closed Mon. rest of year. 596-6457

Owls Head Transportation Museum, rte. 73, 2 miles south of town, exhibits antique aircraft & automobiles. Adm.; open daily May—Oct., Mon.—Fri. rest of year. 594-4418

RUMFORD

Rumford Wild Animal Farm, rte. 2 at Rumford Pt., has animals & birds from around world. Adm.; open daily in summer. 364-7043

SACO

 Aquaboggan, rte. 1 (off I-195), offers waterslides, bumper boats, arcade. Adm.; open daily in summer. 282-3112

Ferry Beach SP, rte. 9 off Bay View Rd., has sandy beaches & nature trails. Adm.; open daily in summer. 283-0067

Funtown USA, rte. 1 (off I-195), is amusement park with rides, including roller coaster & log flume. Adm.; open daily in summer,

weekends only May—mid-June. 284-5139

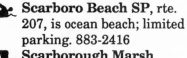 **ME Aquarium**, rte. 1 (off I-195), exhibits local & tropical sea creatures, including eels, sharks, seals, penguins & octopus; education programs, touchable tide pool animals, nature trail. Adm.; open daily year-round. 284-4511

SCARBOROUGH

Scarboro Beach SP, rte. 207, is ocean beach; limited parking. 883-2416

Scarborough Marsh Nature Center, rte. 9, run by ME Audubon Soc., has 3,000-acre salt marsh to explore by foot or canoe, with or without guides. Free visitor center has exhibits & interpretive programs. Fee for canoe rentals & guided tours; open daily in summer. 883-5100

SEARSPORT

Moose Point SP, off rte. 1, offers views of Penobscot Bay, boat launch.

Penobscot Marine Museum, rte. 1 at Church St., displays Down-East sailing art & artifacts in 7 buildings. Adm.; open June—mid-Oct. 548-2529

SKOWHEGAN has one of the oldest fairs in US:

♪ **Lakewood Theatre**, Lake Wesserunsett, 5 miles north of town, draws internationally-known stars for its summer stock; ME state theater.

Margaret Chase Smith Lib. Center, Norridgewock Ave., has slide show, displays of 36-year political career. 474-7133

SOUTH BERWICK

 Vaughan Woods, off rte. 236, is 250-acre forest along banks of Salmon Falls River;

nature trails. Free; open daily in summer. 693-6231

TRENTON
Acadia Zoological Park, rte. 3, is non-profit 100-acre preserve with over 150 animals in petting area. Open daily in summer & early fall. 667-3244
Odyssey Park, rte. 3, offers bumper boats, speed boats, go-carts, bumper cars. Adm.; open daily in summer. 667-5841
Wilderness Park Waterslide, rte. 3, has waterslides, playground, arcade. Adm.; open daily in summer. 667-3573

VAN BUREN
Acadian Village, rte. 1 near Canadian border, has 16 reconstructed buildings to depict early 19th-century life in St. John Valley. Adm.; open daily in summer. 868-2691

WALDOBORO
Waldoboro Museum, rte. 220, consists of schoolhouse, barn with tools & display building with ship models, quilts & handcrafts. Nature trail. Donations; open Tues.—Sun. in summer.

WATERVILLE
Colby College Museum of Art, at Bixler Art & Music Center, exhibits works of ME artists; folk art. Free; open daily except holiday weekends. 872-3228
Cottle's Place, 450 Kennedy Mem. Dr., offers variety of wet & dry slides, bumper boats, jumping pillow, train ride, petting farm, playground. Fee; open daily June—Oct., weekends in May. 872-2304
Redington Museum, 64 Silver St., is replica of 19th-

century apothecary shop, including soda fountain. Kids free; open Tues.-Sat., mid-May—Sept. 872-9439

WELD
Mt. Blue SP, off rte. 156, on Webb Lake, has interpretive program; naturalist leads hikes from camping area. Fee; open mid-May—mid-Oct. 585-2347

WELLS
Laudholm Farm, off rte. 1, offers extensive trail network through 1,500 acres of varied habitats along 9 miles of seashore; visitor center, interpretive programs. Free; hours vary. 646-4521
Rachel Carson Wildlife Refuge, rte. 9, has easy mile-long circular trail through woods, with boardwalk over marsh. Free; open year-round. 646-9064
Wells Antique Auto Museum, rte. 1, exhibits 60 antique & classic autos, including 1904 Stanley Steamer & 1963 Studebaker Skylark; collection of nickelodeons, picture machines & pinball machines; rides in Model T Ford. Adm.; open daily March—Dec., Wed.—Sun. rest of year. 646-9064

WEST PARIS
Perham's of West Paris, rte. 26, a gem & mineral shop, offers free advice & maps to local mineral collecting areas. Free; open daily, March—Dec., Wed.—Sun. rest of year. 674-2341

WOOLWICH
Reid SP, 14 miles south on rte. 127, is popular saltwater park with 1.5 miles of sandy beach, dunes, marshes, ledges. Fee; open daily year-round. 371-2303

YORK BEACH
York's Wild Kingdom, between rtes. 1 & 1A, is zoo & amusement park. Adm.; open daily May—Oct. 363-4911

YORK
Cliff Walk, end of Harbor Beach Rd., is 2-mile trail on cliffs above crashing surf. Free; open year-round.
Old York Hist. Soc., 140 Lindsay Rd. in the George Marshall Store, offers tours conducted by costumed guides; several restored buildings, including schoolhouse & jail. Adm.; open mid-June—Oct. 363-4975
River Walk, off rte. 103, goes along York River & over Wiggly Bridge, a suspension pedestrian bridge overlooking old tidal mill. Free; open year-round.